Are We All Hyperactive?
The Astonishing Epidemic of Attention Disorders

THE SEA HORSE IMPRINT

Paola Mieli, *Publisher & Director*
Mark Stafford, *Editorial Director*
Ona Nierenberg, *Supporting Editor*

This book is published under the aegis and with the financial assistance of
Après-Coup Psychoanalytic Association, New York
and
with the financial support of The Solomon and Gillespie Fund

Cover Image: Detail of Pieter Bruegel the Elder's *Children's Games*, 1560, Kunsthistorisches Museum, Vienna

Patrick Landman

Are We All Hyperactive?
The Astonishing Epidemic of Attention Disorders

Translated by Peter Gillespie and David Jacobson

Foreword by Allen Frances

Agincourt Press
New York, 2024

Originally published in French as *Tous hyperactifs ? : L'incroyable épidémie de troubles de l'attention*, Éditions Albin Michel, 2015.

© 2024 by Sea Horse Imprint

ISBN: 978-1-946328-38-0

Copyediting
Hilary Ilkay

Design and typesetting
Danilo Montanari

Agincourt Press
P.O. Box 1039
Cooper Station
New York, NY 10003
www.agincourtbooks.com

The publisher welcomes enquiries from copyright-holders he has been unable to contact.

To Dominique, my spouse
To Luc, Patricia, Valérie, Raphaël, Élise, and Jonathan,
my children and their partners
To Eva, Quentin, and Chloé, my grandchildren
To my father Philippe Landman
To my brother Claude Landman

Table of Contents

Foreword

It is a great pleasure for me to introduce you to this interesting and richly documented book, in which my dear friend Patrick Landman, child psychiatrist, psychoanalyst, jurist and cosmopolitan Parisian, presents different ways to avoid the over-diagnosis of Attention Deficit Hyperactivity Disorder (ADHD) and its treatment through stimulants. Far from remaining within the narrow confines of a purely descriptive psychiatric approach, this book represents a valuable contribution that draws upon European clinical psychopathology and a bio-psycho-social model of the mind and mental illness. It adopts a practical rather than ideological perspective.

The over-diagnosis of ADHD and its chemical treatment is a serious problem. In the U.S., cases have increased threefold in just twenty years, leaving our children outright addicts to medications. Today, 11 percent of children aged 4-17 are diagnosed with ADHD and 6 percent are treated with medication. And the percentage reaches vertiginous figures for teenage males: 20 percent are diagnosed and 10 percent are treated. Hopefully Dr. Landman's book will help safeguard France from the temptation to follow the American example of excessive diagnosis of ADHD and culpable negligence in assessment and treatment.

The bewildering explosion of ADHD in the United States can be explained as follows: either it was previously under-diagnosed, and this increased awareness can account for most of the new cases; or it is now over-diagnosed, an outcome that is widely encouraged by the pharmaceutical industry; or it is a combination of both factors.

Undoubtedly the increase in this diagnosis may be partly due to better screening of actual cases. But we have massive evidence that what we are witnessing today is a passing fad that has largely been created by the commercial practices of the pharmaceutical industry and facilitated by the laxity of prescribing physicians. It is noteworthy that the most reliable predicting factor in the possible identification of ADHD today is the child's date of birth: the probability of getting a diagnosis of ADHD is almost doubled for the youngest child in a classroom compared with the oldest! An uncertain diagnosis has transformed ordinary immaturity at a given age into a psychiatric disorder treated with medication instead of simply letting the child grow up...

It is also no coincidence that rates began to skyrocket immediately after three unrelated events that occurred almost simultaneously in the United States in the late 1990s.

First, new drugs patented to treat attention deficit disorder came on the market. They were no more effective than the old ones, but they were much more expensive, providing both the means and the opportunity for aggressive marketing, which worked very well. Twenty years ago, sales of ADHD drugs were a modest $40 million; today they have skyrocketed to an obscene $10 billion. Wouldn't it be better to spend much of that money on something other than drugs? For example, by reducing class sizes and increasing the number of gym hours so that restless kids can let off steam?

Second event: the U.S. Food and Drug Administration authorized pharmaceutical companies to conduct advertising campaigns aimed directly at the consumer. These companies quickly came to the conclusion that the royal road to a skyrocketing market for their expensive new pills was to popularize ADHD. And they spread the misleading message that ADHD is extremely common, frequently under-diagnosed, and the cause of all school and behavioral problems resulting from a chemical imbalance that is easily treated with medication. Marketing was targeted at general practitioners, who nowadays make up the bulk of psychotropic drug prescribers. Seeing children in their worst light, they write out – most of the time after too short a consultation – quick and needless prescriptions. However, children change considerably from one month to the next, without intervention, and they are the most difficult patients to diagnose. Pharmaceutical treatment should be used only as a last resort for the most obvious, harmful and persistent disorders. Yet medications are often prescribed without precaution – almost like candy.

Third event: the first report of a multicentric study widely distributed to the public suggested that drug treatment was superior to psychotherapy for ADHD. Yet further follow-up studies showed no long-term effectiveness of drug treatment on educational outcomes, but they received little attention.

It is easy to over-diagnose and over-treat ADHD. It is defined by non-specific symptoms and behaviors widely distributed across the general population: poor concentration, distraction, impulsiveness and hyperactivity. At the extremes, the diagnosis is easy to make. It is impossible to make a mistake when a child has classic, severe early ADHD, while at the other extreme most children clearly do not have ADHD. But between the two poles, within flexible, blurred and densely populated boundaries, it is difficult to distinguish between children diagnosed with ADHD and children who are nothing but lively and hard to control.

Some 2 to 4 percent of children could probably justify a diagnosis of ADHD and probably many of them could benefit from drug treatment – at least in the short term. But the actual current rate of consumption of medications, which is steadily increasing worldwide, makes no sense.

Let us hope that Patrick Landman's book will alert us to these abuses.

Allen Frances, MD
Professor Emeritus of Psychiatry
Duke University, Durham, North Carolina

Preface by the Author to the English Edition

When I wrote this book eight years ago, I sensed that an epidemic was about to break out in France, that of ADD/ADHD. All the ingredients needed to trigger it were present: a disorder present in the DSM, whose boundaries with the norm were blurred and ill-defined, and whose inclusion threshold was relatively low; a disorder centered on a crucial cognitive function and constituting a prerequisite for success at school, academically and professionally, namely attention; and finally, a remedy in the form of a drug that worked.

The pharmaceutical laboratories had prepared the ground by funding a parents' association promoting ADHD.

The only parameter limiting the epidemic explosion was the influence and historical place of psychoanalysis in French child psychiatry. Psychoanalysts rejected the diagnosis of ADD/ADHD. They considered attention deficit disorder and hyperactivity to be symptoms of psychological suffering in children, the reasons for which were not to be found in cerebral dysfunction alone, and they opposed the commonplace prescription of psychotropic drugs in children. In France, psychoanalysts had built a dam against the influence of biological-behavioral psychiatry on child psychiatry.

In the field of autism, however, a series of well-constructed media campaigns, combined with effective lobbying, had enabled parents' associations — some of which could be described as activist, others as very active — to discredit psychoanalysis as dogmatic, outdated and unscientific. In these campaigns, it was said, not without reason but with great excess, that psychoanalysts had failed in the treatment of infantile autism by emphasizing parental and more particularly maternal etiology, that they were sectarian in their thinking and refused to evaluate their therapeutic methods.

ADD/ADHD promoters imitated the autistic parents' associations, but ADD/ADHD suffered from two difficulties in its promotion:

firstly, until version 5 of the DSM, ADD/ADHD was considered a behavioral disorder, and it was rightly suspected of being pharmaco-induced, thus playing into Big Pharma's hands.

These two difficulties have faded with the inclusion of ADHD in DSM-5 as part of a vast group of neuro-developmental disorders, and the reluctance to prescribe psychotropic drugs has diminished as the influence of psychoanalysis and knowledge of psychopathology has diminished among new generations of child psychiatrists.

Today, the ADD/ADHD epidemic is well established in France.

Over-diagnosis of ADHD and over-prescription have become the rule.

There is, however, one parameter that I had completely overlooked eight years ago. It's called the "augmented child."

Since neuroscience and cognitive science have become dominant, psychiatry has tended to become organ medicine, the medicine of one organ, the brain, to the point where there no longer seems to be much to separate psychiatry from neurology. All mental disorders are considered to involve the brain, all the more so in the developing child.

Today, there is a widespread scientific, reductionist belief in brain imaging as the microscope of the 21st century, which some refer to as "neuromania."

But in the case of ADD/ADHD, this neuromania intersects with another phenomenon that has emerged: improvement medicine. We need to go beyond therapeutic medicine to practice improvement medicine.

This is a new trend that is gathering pace, particularly in the field of cognitive performance. In some cases, ADD/ADHD is becoming a cover for improving a child's attention and, consequently, school performance. It's not just a drug that's being prescribed, but a kind of school, academic or professional dopant, which encourages the epidemic. Such prescriptions can make invisible the social factors and psychological suffering that lead children and their families to seek help.

ADHD is becoming the leading cause of consultation in child psychiatry. It is also making headway in adult psychiatry.

Paradoxically, it's not impossible that ADD/ADHD will become less and less useful in a society where improving cognitive performance with the help of medication is considered the rule, as part of mental health and no longer just psychiatry.

We'll go from "All Hyperactive" to "All Cognitively Augmented" to "All Artificially Intelligent."

Patrick Landman
June 2023

Introduction

"Your daughter has ADHD," "I'm an adult with ADHD," "My client has a mental illness that may lessen his responsibility: ADHD." In medical, pediatric, child psychiatric, psychiatric, and even courthouse settings, there is increasing talk of "Attention Deficit Disorder with or without hyperactivity."

Without getting into polemics about the methods, diagnostic criteria, or reference classifications used, it is notable that France stands at the bottom of the scale of Western countries in its percentage of those diagnosed with ADHD within the general population. According to the 2011 Lecendreux study, its prevalence for children aged 6 to 12 years is around 3.5 percent.[1] Yet we're sure to see an epidemic of attention deficit disorder with or without hyperactivity, and this book will explain the reasons that lead me to predict this though I've never claimed to have the slightest gift of prophecy.

It's as fascinating as it is worrisome to explore how a pseudo-mental illness fits into the field of public health and comes to be seen as a serious public health problem. We have precedent such as the outbreak of depression in the 1980s, when the *Diagnostic and Statistical Manual of Mental Disorders III* medicalized affects and behaviors such as sadness, low self-esteem or attachment dependency, whereas these are usual reactions to breakups or failures and are spontaneously reversible. Once the DSM-III lowered the inclusion thresholds, a considerable number of these normal reactions were diagnosed as a "major depressive episode." False depressives were treated, sometimes for very long periods of time, and depression came to

---

[1] Stephen V. Faraone, Michel Lecendreux, and Eric Konofal. "Growth Dysregulation and ADHD: An Epidemiologic Study of Children in France," *Journal of Attention Disorders* 16, no. 7 (Oct. 2012), 572-8, https://www.researchgate.net/publication/51547728.

be called the "Disease of the Century."[2] The same has been true of bipolar disorder in recent decades. All it took was the invention of a pseudo-cycle of moods, with no scientific basis, for us to go from manic-depressive psychosis — which affects a minority of the population — to "everyone is bipolar!"

It's quite hard to explain why we got here. It is urgent, though, to understand these fads and their participants — scientists, users, patients, doctors, merchants, industrialists — be they honest, naïve, manipulated or predatory.

When I speak of pseudo-disease or pseudo-illness in relation to ADHD, someone can rightly rebut that most mental illnesses are pseudo-illnesses: after all, wasn't Charcot's notorious hysteria just a pseudo-disease, or Freud's famous obsessional neurosis? The proof is that they've been replaced by TAG,[3] OCD and other disorders such as fibromyalgia[4], tetany[5], etc. There is a great fluctuation in what we call mental illnesses. Their manifestation and naming aren't fixed or objectifiable; they vary according to cultures and eras; they are social constructs. Subjects marginalized by their suffering or mental illness use the forms available to them from the surrounding culture to express their symptoms: Claude Lévi-Strauss spoke of "floating signifiers" in a society, at the disposal of suffering subjects waiting to be dealt with.[6] But the way in which medicine names these symptoms and the explanatory hypotheses it provides aren't all equivalent. Some hypotheses are useful for the ailing subject. By alleviating suffering, they bring progress to culture. For instance, Freud's discovery and his interest in the so-called talking cure was probably an artifact produced between Breuer, Freud and the patient known as Anna O. Nevertheless, giving

---

[2] This claim is widespread but its origin is obscure. See for example: Erica da Silva et al., "Pharmaceutical Attention to the Risks of Inappropriate Use of Marijuana in the Treatment of Depression," *Research, Society and Development* 11, no. 17 (2022). The article is typical in that it repeats the claim, "Depression is the disease of the century, as some call it" without citation.

[3] The acronym for Talented and Gifted.

[4] Fibromyalgia is a disorder of the sensory activity of the nervous system characterized by widespread muscle pain, joint stiffness and fatigue. The condition is chronic but pain can come and go and moves about the body.

[5] Tetany is either a sudden and continuous involuntary contraction of a muscle or group of muscles or a steady contraction of a muscle without distinct twitching.

[6] Claude Lévi-Strauss, *Introduction to Marcel Mauss*, trans. Felicity Baker (London: Routledge, 1987).

"hysterical" women a voice and especially listening to them – because they possessed knowledge – rather than judging them or considering them to be malingerers, marked a cultural advance, and a liberating step forward, perhaps, in the condition of women.

What about ADHD? Does the promotion of ADHD represent progress for unstable, inattentive, impulsive children, "flaky" and distracted teenagers, or adults with their head in the clouds? Should we be alarmed by what may be a simple change of signifiers, a different expression of rationality, under the impact of neuroscience and the study of the brain? Should we be so focused on one or two behavioral symptoms, without considering context, as the DSM-5 advises? Should we reduce all clinical pictures of attention deficit and hyperactivity to neurobiological dysfunction, independent of environmental, psychological and social factors? To what extent should the hyperactive child's interaction with his or her parents be addressed? Should we be satisfied with providing behavioral advice, parenting education, and advice on healthy living, or isn't our role to try to shed light on the family's psychic economy, on the child's phantasmatic position and parental projections, on prohibitions and their limits? Should we be interested in the psychic structure of the child; the manifestations of reactive hyperactivity; neurotic or psychotic restlessness, or one revealing a borderline state? Or should we be satisfied with an overall diagnosis of ADHD? When and how should hyperactive or ADHD children be treated? Should their treatment be only chemical or should it be accompanied by support services, and if so, which ones? Does ADHD reveal new mental health actors as users?

The list of questions could be longer still, but I'll try to answer the ones above, since this book isn't just an attempt at denunciation, but is also meant to be constructive. However, on the precise point of knowing whether or not promoting ADHD has been beneficial, I would answer no, even if in some areas it's helped to better identify certain issues.

I'm pessimistic about the long-range impact of promoting ADHD and will try to show the reasons why. In Chapter 1, I'll give a brief summary of the evolving psychiatric setting in which the notion of ADHD was born and developed. In Chapter 2, I'll discuss the polemics surrounding ADHD, which include quarrels among experts as well as social and public health questions. I'll also show how European clinicians have transitioned from their model of the "unstable child" to American psychiatry's ADHD diagnosis, which is dominated by biomedical paradigms. In Chapter 3, I'll address the general problem of diagnosis in psychiatry. In Chapter 4, I'll present the arguments of ADHD advocates before refuting them. Chapter 5 will be devoted to the psychoanalytic approach to hyperactivity. In Chapter 6, I'll discuss new therapeutic methods and confounding factors that bias diagnosis. In chapter 7, I'll question Big Pharma's psycho-marketing and its method of promoting new mental illnesses. Chapter 8 will describe "neuromania," to borrow an English-language term, and its impact on the spread of ADHD. In chapter 9, I'll introduce the notion of evidence-based practice that has revolutionized medicine and present its problematic application to psychiatry, which the instance of ADHD illustrates perfectly. In the last chapter, I'll return to ADHD in the strict sense of the term to talk more precisely about the diagnosis of ADHD in adolescents and adults, since both have advanced in their own way and carry their own specific risks. Finally, I'll conclude by taking a stance on the very existence of ADHD.

Chapter 1: From the "Unstable Child" to ADHD

The restless child seems to be of increasing concern to mental health professionals and officials. Over the past 30 years, restlessness in children has been the object of more and more frequent messages from researchers, psychologists, clinicians and psychiatrists around the world, with a convergence that has gradually evolved into a consensus on the existence of a "disease" called ADHD. This "disease" is on an inexorable rise: the latest data in the United States show more than 11 percent of American children aged 6 to 17 years suffering from ADHD.[7]

The purpose of this book can be summed up in one question: does ADHD exist? This question appears to us to be urgent for multiple overlapping reasons. Above all, by a sort of contagious effect, the focus of the scientific psychiatric community has shifted from the restlessness of the child to that of the adolescent and then that of the adult (elderly subjects are spared for the moment). In order to be able to extend this "disease" to all (or almost all) of the population, it's been necessary to change a few of its components. The main motivation for this change has been the unremarked upon association established between "attention" and "restlessness." In effect, if all children are restless to varying degrees – just like young mammals, kittens or puppies, for example – the same doesn't hold true for teenagers, let alone adults. But by associating attention and agitation, and especially by assigning the leading role to attention, the extension from one to the other is made easier. Indeed, it's quite rare to meet adults who have the sort of incessant motor agitation that children do, who can't keep still, who move about inappropriately and excessively, and in doing so annoy their family and other close company. Such cases exist, as we know from the documentation of certain neurological diseases.

---

[7] See: www.cdc.gov/ncbddd/adhd.

But, outside this framework, motor agitation in adults is most often sequential and a reaction to situations of stress, violent shocks, trauma or prolonged confinement. In other words, to extrapolate infantile restlessness to the adult condition is practically impossible or at the very least risky. Put the focus on attention, however, and all the facts of the problem change, because if agitation in the motor sense – known in medical language as hyperkinesia – is rare in adults, the same isn't true of attention disorders. What adult doesn't suffer at some point from trouble with attention? To be prone to distraction is part of everyday life, as is forgetting certain objects or events. With this association between attention/hyperactivity, the restless child and the distractible adult are likely, under certain conditions, of course, to come under the rubric of ADHD. And teenagers? An adolescent may be fidgety like a child or absent-minded like an adult, or both together.

In reality, ADHD isn't based just on symptoms of agitation and deficient attention: there's a third component, which is impulsiveness. While restlessness and poor concentration (distractibility) exist in adolescents, they are neither characteristic of this age group nor especially frequent, whereas impulsiveness is much more common. Indeed, teenagers are often provocative, thoughtless, and generally more likely to commit a *passage-à-l'acte* (that is, pathological triggering of an impulsive, violent action)[8] than adults; and we can see in this the characteristics of impulsiveness, at least to some degree. So the restless child, the impulsive adolescent and the easily distracted adult, as well as certain combinations such as the easily distracted and restless teenager or the easily distracted and impulsive adult, can potentially be diagnosed with ADHD. Another advantage of *not* focusing on hyperkinesia is that the female population is less likely to be restless or impulsive while, according to some studies, more likely to be "internally distracted" and "intellectually impaired."[9] Consequently,

---

[8] *Passage à l'acte* (passage to the act) is a concept taken from French psychiatry designating the point when the subject proceeds from an idea or intention to the corresponding act, oftentimes of an aggressive, violent or criminal nature directed toward themself or others. It is considered a possible mark of the onset of a psychotic episode. Lacan goes beyond this description and defines *passage à l'acte* as the moment in which the subject, in an attempt to escape an experience of anguish that otherwise cannot be bound or displaced, attempts to dissolve their subjectivity and social bonds through the act.

[9] E. Mark Mahone and Ericka L. Wodka, "The Neurobiological Profile of Girls with ADHD," *Developmental Disabilities Research Reviews* 14 (2008), 276-284.

adapting and reprioritizing the criteria of the DSM schema in this way automatically ensnares more females into the ever-widening net of the ADHD diagnosis.[10]

But before the risk of ADHD could be extended to the vast majority of the population, it was necessary to convince the scientific community that ADHD exists. This was no easy task, since psychiatry is a special branch of medicine. As a general rule, in medicine, the knowledge of a new disease or novel syndrome is the result of a discovery, one which may bear the name of its discoverer, such as amyotrophic lateral sclerosis (which in France is called Charcot's disease, whereas in the U.S. it's known as Lou Gehrig's disease, thus named for one of its casualties) or, to give another example, Sydenham chorea disease. There are many examples that illustrate the scientific method at work in medical research. A scientist discovers a *syndrome*, that is, a non-fortuitous grouping of signs, which enables the search for a cause, because every syndrome has one or more causes.

Similarly, and with even stronger force of example, a scientist discovers a *disease*, and this disease has a causal agent, which is the etiology of that disease.[11] Once the causal agent (a bacterium or a virus) has been identified, research can be methodically oriented toward potential treatments: for instance, by injecting the causal agent into an animal and making it a carrier of this disease, and by comparing the effect of different results, different products, on the evolution of the disease. Discovering the causative agent of a disease is a fundamental step toward understanding pathological mechanisms. It generally opens the door to discovering other causative agents for comparable diseases; it advances medicine as a whole and not just the treatment of the disease of which the causative agent has been discovered. Sometimes the medical discovery may come out of chance circumstances that uncover something other than what was being searched for. But

---

[10] There is a concerted effort to close the gender gap. Accordingly, "subtle" clinical examples have been discovered in girls such as "internalized distraction," which conflates the clear behavioral signs of inattention with a strictly psychological condition. Also, because girls seem to exhibit the symptomatic criteria for ADHD at a later age, the DSM-5 raised the onset of the disorder from 7 to 12 years old, which automatically raised the rate of diagnosis among girls. [Translators' note]

[11] A disease is a disorder of the body's structure or function that has a known cause and a distinctive group of symptoms. A syndrome, on the other hand, is a collection of symptoms that frequently appear together without an identifiable cause.

this doesn't take anything away from the method itself, which remains rational, ultimately identifying a cause and its effects.

Notably, the course of events is totally different for psychiatry, and has been ever since its birth. Therefore, we must briefly review some historical elements to better trace the origins of what is at stake today, in particular in relation to the questions concerning ADHD, because the present situation cannot be understood without observing that it is the culmination of a certain history.

Western medicine has undergone a long historical development, beginning with ancient Greece.[12] Some medical historians even claim that medical discourse was established and formulated by Hippocrates, therefore long before medicine used the scientific method. Certainly the history of medicine has not been linear, but the fact that each future physician has to pledge an oath on Hippocrates' text, even if it primarily has the symbolic value of an initiation rite, nevertheless links the future physician to a certain history and perhaps even more so to a certain discourse and its supposed origins. Medicine became scientific only in the course of the 19th century, with great discoveries such as those of Pasteur. Though not everything in medicine is scientific, the scientific method plays a preponderant role. Can the same be said of psychiatry? Truth be told, it doesn't seem so. It's true that ancient medicine, Hebrew or Greek, and in particular Hippocrates, designated diseases of the soul which it explained with causal theories that were partly theological or philosophical. However, psychiatry no longer refers to this origin because it underwent a radical transformation in the 19th century. With the arrival of the Enlightenment in the 18th century, reason triumphed over faith. In European societies, and a little later in the United States, those considered to be "reasonable people" would take to locking up so-called unreasonable or insane people: it was the epoch of asylum building. Michel Foucault speaks of this "great confinement" and of psychiatry as the monologue of "reasonable people about unreasonable ones."[13] This thesis has been contested by various historians of psychiatry, in particular Edward

---

[12] Of course, concerning origins, we could also mention other traditions such as ancient Hebrew and Chinese medicine among others.

[13] Michel Foucault, *Madness and Civilization: A History of Insanity in the Age of Reason,* trans. Richard Howard (New York: Vintage-Random House, 1988).

Shorter[14] or Gladys Swain and Marcel Gauchet,[15] and the dispute has itself been the subject of pertinent criticism by Élisabeth Roudinesco.[16] But regardless of one's position on this debate, this period would profoundly mark the history of psychiatry, because if "surveillance" and the custody of the insane were to be delegated to doctors, it was not *mainly* for scientific reasons but for the sake of social and public order. Psychiatry has remained tainted by this original mark. And psychiatrists have therefore long felt devalued in relation to other doctors who accused them of being "alienists," of practicing unscientific medicine.

Things changed with the arrival of neuroleptics and, later, other psychotropic drugs. Psychiatrists gained access to effective medications that enabled improvements in the conditions of care and the lives of the chronically mentally ill. Psychiatry entered a new era: that of psychopharmacology. Psychiatry's view of symptoms also gradually changed: the traditional clinic, which was based on observation and metapsychological theoretical hypotheses, particularly those stemming from psychoanalysis, gradually gave way to another one – a clinic dominated by pharmacology. Symptoms became classified more and more according to the actions of medications. For instance, an anxiety that responds to antidepressants would no longer be considered an acute anxiety or acute anxiety state, but a state of panic, in contrast to a chronic anxiety that responds to anxiolytics[17] and is called "generalized anxiety disorder" in the DSM. This change of name is not insignificant, because previously, the clinic centered on the affect, that is to say, on the anxiety that was either acute or chronic: the patient suffered from acute anxiety attacks and/or chronic anxiety. Henceforth, there exists only a state of panic or a "generalized anxiety disorder" depending solely on the patient's response to a particular type of medication. Pharmacological action would not only contribute to improving the care of the mentally ill and redrawing the clinic as well as nosography (that is, the classification of mental disorders), but it would also con-

---

[14] Edward Shorter, *A History of Psychiatry: From the Era of the Asylum to the Age of Prozac* (New York: John Wiley and Sons, 1998).

[15] Gladys Swain and Marcel Gauchet, *Le Sujet de la folie* (Paris: Calmann-Lévy, 1997).

[16] Elisabeth Roudinesco, *Philosophes dans la tourmente* (Paris: Fayard, 2005).

[17] Anxiolytics are drugs (such as Benzodiazepines) that are used to prevent and treat anxiety disorders.

tribute to spreading false reasoning that can be formulated in these terms: if a medication alleviates symptoms or makes them disappear, it means that the symptoms were the result of a so-called chemical imbalance, which the drug is supposed to repair. Subsequently, this reasoning was overexploited by biological psychiatry to justify the need for prescriptions. We have witnessed a whole set of hypotheses concerning purported chemical imbalances in the field of psychiatry, all of them risky and false. We can cite the dopaminergic[18] hypothesis for schizophrenia – the hypothesis that schizophrenia is due to a deficit in dopamine, a neuromediator[19] – or the hypothesis that depression is related to a deficit in serotonin. The latest imbalance in vogue concerns oxytocin in which low levels of the natural hormone are oftentimes correlated with several disorders (such as depression, anorexia nervosa and autism spectrum disorder) without any causal link having been established.[20] This reasoning leads to the inference of a hierarchy of therapeutic modalities in which drug prescription plays the key role. In fact, if a mental disorder is thought to be linked to a chemical deficit, the first recourse is logically constituted by providing the chemical that is lacking or by restoring biological balance.[21] While this doesn't bar other interventions such as psychotherapy, these non-pharmacological interventions are now conceived as peripheral, ancillary or comingled. After all, a diabetic patient may need psychotherapy; yet who would dare to claim that psychotherapy is a cure for diabetes or that it's necessary in all cases? Everyone knows that the

---

[18] Dopaminergic refers to the release or administering of dopamine as a neurotransmitter. Drugs with this effect are commonly used in the treatment of schizophrenia.

[19] A neuromediator is a chemical molecule naturally produced in the body (such as adrenaline, dopamine and serotonin) that is responsible for transmitting messages between neurons.

[20] Oxytocin is a natural hormone and a neurotransmitter that is involved in childbirth and breastfeeding, facilitating contraction and lactation. It is sometimes referred to as the "love hormone," because levels of oxytocin increase during sexual activity.

[21] Recently, some leaders in the field of psychiatry have overturned the "chemical imbalance" theory. See for example: Joanna Moncrieff, Ruth C. Cooper, Tom Stockmann et al. "The Serotonin Theory of Depression: A Systematic Umbrella Review of the Evidence," *Molecular Psychiatry* (2022). This study concluded, "Our comprehensive review of the major strands of research on serotonin shows there is no convincing evidence that depression is associated with, or caused by, lower serotonin concentrations or activity." Definitive studies like this one have, unfortunately, only shifted the focus onto other biological deterministic theories such as brain dysfunction and genetic predisposition.

proper treatment for diabetes is insulin. Rather than keeping on top of advances in science, a whole current of psychiatry has jumbled speculation, hypotheses and validated scientific facts. Curiously, among psychiatrists and researchers in psychiatry during the last decades of the 20th century and the first decade of the 21st, we have witnessed a flourishing of the phenomena of belief. No longer satisfied with facts, we now see false interpretations as well as theories developed under the effect of religious enthusiasm that are presented to the public as scientifically validated with the complicity of doctors, particularly in the field of genetics. This creates media postings like the following: "A rare genetic flaw that occurs spontaneously during development may sharply increase the risk that a child will develop autism,"[22] or "geneticists uncover a key clue to schizophrenia."[23]

Nevertheless, science is advancing in its knowledge of the brain, and the more it advances, the more complex the research becomes, because the brain delivers up its secrets only in small drops. This, without a doubt, is one of the greatest scientific adventures of the coming century. We can therefore understand certain anticipatory formulations of some of those taking part in this adventure. But parallel with these entirely understandable anticipations are theories that aim to explain all mental illnesses by brain dysfunction. They are reductionist theories, in the sense that they reduce a mental fact to a neuronal event. In this paradigm, mental illnesses are conceived solely as neurological illnesses; psychic reality is erased, denied, and subjective experience is secondary, just as it is in organic illnesses.

ADHD partakes of this reductionist tendency. From the outset and without any evidence, proponents of ADHD have considered hy-

---

[22] Benedict Carey, "Scientists Link Gene Mutation to Autism Risk," *The New York Times*, April 4, 2012. The article provides an important qualification that undermines the claim made in the title, "The gene mutations are extremely rare and together account for a tiny fraction of autism cases – in these studies, only a handful of children."

[23] Melissa Healy, "Geneticists Uncover a Key Clue to Schizophrenia," *The Los Angeles Times*, Jan. 27, 2016. The article states, "The study offers the first clear evidence of a neurobiological basis for a disease," but ends with a quote from a geneticist from Emory University contradicting this claim, "Clearly the [variant of the C4 gene] explanation does not fully explain schizophrenia risk, and it is also clear that genetic variation alone is insufficient to solely cause schizophrenia." For a comprehensive study of the media's propensity to promote the genetic cause of mental illness see: Peter Conrad, "Genetic Optimism: Framing Genes and Mental Illness in the News," *Culture, Medicine and Psychiatry* 25, no. 2 (2001), 225-47.

peractive children as suffering from a brain lesion that is qualified as minimal. Subsequently, this thesis has become a credo while being substantiated only by correlations. A certain number of studies have shown evidence of modification of brain development and brain functioning in children labeled with ADHD compared to so-called normal children. These visible modifications in brain imaging, however, don't prove the existence of ADHD but only correlations between brain changes and behavioral symptoms. It's surprising that disturbed or restless children have abnormal brain images, but it's important to note that these studies are not yet able to draw the distinction between brain abnormalities, delayed development or mere immaturity. In other words, not only do these images not constitute evidence, but they also highlight a major confounding factor[24] in the diagnosis of ADHD: *immaturity*. We'll come back to these brain-imaging studies in Chapter 8, but for now we can already mention a number of problems related to their use and especially their interpretation. To start with, there is a general tendency toward establishing causal connections with the use of images. This tendency is clearly on display with the *La preuve par l'image* competition inaugurated in 2010 by AFCAS (French-Canadian Association for the Advancement of Science).[25] Their slogan is, "take science from the other end of the telescope starting from the image and not from words" and their goal is to facilitate scientific dialogue with the general public to "make clear that science is not an expense but an investment."[26] Therefore "proof by the image" is the supreme proof where conviction can hold sway — *not* in science. However, as with all images, brain-imaging scans don't necessarily speak for themselves. They need to be interpreted, and interpretation is more important than the image itself. Yet if an interpretation is often correct when reading studies in publications intended for the general public, we can observe a disturbing sleight of hand taking place: particular hypotheses are unwisely (and abusively) raised to the level of scien-

---

[24] A confounding factor is a variable that masks an actual association or falsely demonstrates an apparent association between the study variables where no real association between them exists. If confounding factors are not taken into account, bias may result in the conclusions of the study.

[25] Proof by the image. [Translators' note]

[26] For more information on this competition see: https://www.acfas.ca/prix-concours/preuve-image. For the cited slogan see: https://www.concours-preuve-image.fr/a-propos/.

tifically-proven certainties; correlations between certain behavioral symptoms and regions of the brain are presented as evidence of the location of "the disease." This inexorably leads to the "logical" inference of its cause, which is invariably supposed to be of organic origin. In this context, we cannot forget that there is currently *no biological marker for any of the major mental illnesses*, be it schizophrenia, autism or one of the bipolar disorders. Renaming them as neurodevelopmental diseases or disorders does not change that fact. The problem is exacerbated when scientists, who are clinical researchers themselves, conform to expectations, driven by various motives: promotion of their research, matters of belief, attempts to influence public health policies or the desire to meet the aspirations of patients, patient associations or patients' parents. Lastly, there are conflicts of interest with the pharmaceutical industry as has been proved in the United States (unfortunately for some). It is evident that "proof by the image" of a so-called exclusive organic causality almost automatically leads to the opportunity, more often the necessity, to resort to medications. This renders essential psychotherapeutic and social interventions secondary, even superfluous, leading to a lack of interest in these approaches on the part of professionals (especially psychiatrists) and therefore to a gap in their training.

These approaches are sometimes reduced to stereotypes like "educational advice" or "guidelines for healthy living." Such advice is far from useless but it can't replace the singular therapeutic dialogue between a subject, their parents perhaps, and a mental health professional trained to elicit subjective speech. However, only the behaviorist approach to therapy survives, with its collection of standardized data and famous checklists, particularly those of the DSM (which may have their usefulness for medication research or epidemiology, but are totally reductive in clinical practice with patients).

It's not a matter of imposing a psychoanalytical investigation on everyone – especially on those who don't want it. Nor it is a question of considering that a child is always made mentally ill by its social environment, or even of making that environment always responsible for the situation. In my family practice, for instance, I've seen three children who were developing normally while a fourth was suffering from autism. Nothing in the family's history could reasonably explain this drama. Is it the same with ADHD? The parents certainly don't bear responsibility for the disorder, but they do interact with the hyperactive child, and their interactions are not solely conscious. A child always has a place in the parental imaginary. He or she is the object of projections on the part of the parents and these projections have their impact on the child's mental development.

The informed practitioner, aware of an individual or family psychopathology, will be able to tactfully collect data useful for the individualized care of the child, without being limited to providing general advice focused on behaviors and behavioral interactions. For example, while I don't dispute the usefulness of what is called "parenting skills training" or "therapeutic education," these interventions are insufficient and shouldn't be an end in themselves. Rather, whenever possible, they should be considered a stage in care or a complement to a psychotherapeutic or systemic approach. Some patients or families may respond positively to these therapeutic methods, superficial though they may seem. Yet in the name of what moral principle or imperative should we take offence at them? These behaviorist methods don't infringe on medical ethics, and if patients are content with them, there is nothing to be said. The question does not reside there, even if sometimes it seems to be posed in terms that suggest that certain practitioners condemn these methods in the name of psychoanalytic superiority.

To my mind, the main issue is the training, the formation, of practitioners. Since the 1980s and the advent of the American classification of mental disorders called DSM-III, we have seen the one-way orientation of psychiatric education in the West gather force. Simultaneously, explanatory theories about mental difficulties and disorders are on the decline, considered obsolete and unscientific. I'm referring here to psychoanalytic as well as systemic theories, talk psychotherapies or those that question the role of the psychiatric institution such as institutional psychotherapy or the de-institutionalization movement. The paradigms previously given pride of place, such as psychic reality, the search for causes, family dynamics, the unconscious and transference have been replaced by a single, biomedical paradigm and an entirely descriptive psychiatry. The effect of this major overhaul, over the course of thirty years, has been to render the know-how of clinicians useless, and, above all, to make its transmission pointless. This wouldn't have mattered if patients had been better cared for over the last thirty years, if the dominance of biological–behavioral psychiatry had brought about a significant improvement in the condition of patients with acute, temporary or long-term mental illnesses — but that isn't the case. And the country where this psychiatry has been most widely deployed, namely the United States, is seeing an explosion in the use of psychotropic drugs and a steady increase in the number of chronically disabled psychiatric patients. We are seeing more and more "false positives," that is, people wrongly included in mental pathology even though their behavior falls within the variations of normal.

We will have the opportunity to return to these data, but already we can state that ADHD is a perfect illustration of the misguided excesses of biological-behavioral psychiatry and of psychiatry's evolution in general. In thirty years, we have in fact gone from a symptom, namely hyperactivity (whose sought-after multiple triggering factors and various contexts for appearing are sometimes mistakenly confused with causality) to a so-called syndrome — or even a disease — which has an epidemic-like evolution. And all this against the backdrop of the "success" of a molecule, methylphenidate.[27]

---

[27] Methylphenidate is a central nervous system stimulant and the active ingredient in the brand name medications Ritalin and Concerta that are most often prescribed for patients diagnosed with ADHD.

Chapter 2: Psychiatry and Medicine

To explain and look for the cause of diseases and take the usual medical approach to treat them is a multi-phased operation, involving essentially four moments of progression.

First of all, you isolate a syndrome. Etymologically, "syndrome" designates "a running together." A syndrome is defined when you notice a regularity in the symptoms and their changes over time. This regularity suggests that we're in the presence of a specific disease. The second phase consists of identifying a physiopathology, that is, the disclosure of all the physiological and biological mechanisms by which a disease emerges and, in the case of chronic diseases, by which it continues its progression. Then comes the discovery of a treatment that aims to halt or even reverse the physiopathological process. The final phase is the work of prevention, aimed at finding the way or ways to keep the disease from reappearing. All these phases are not always carried out in the same order. It may happen, for instance, that the treatment is discovered before the physiopathological mechanisms have been elucidated. But these four phases constitute a pattern of logical progression, even if their order doesn't always correspond to reality.

Can this pattern be applied to psychiatry, to mental illness, and in particular to the ADHD we're dealing with? Many years ago, tertiary syphilis was considered a mental illness. About 20-25 percent of patients in psychiatric hospitals had it. However, over the past sixty years, neurosyphilis was eradicated once the causal agent, *Treponema pallidum*, was discovered, along with antibiotic treatment. Preventive measures followed. Can we imagine that one day it will be the same for schizophrenia, bipolar disorders or ADHD? This is the hope some people put in medical research. But, in the case of neurosyphilis, can we speak of elucidating the physiological mechanisms of a mental illness? Wasn't it, rather, a matter of elucidating the mechanisms of an infectious physical disease, misdiagnosed as mental?

Numerous objections can be made against applying this model to mental illness. Some opponents of the medical model have taken an extremist position. The most famous of them, Thomas Szasz of the State University of New York Upstate Medical University, called mental illness a myth in his acclaimed book *The Myth of Mental Illness*.[28] This qualification – even if one argues, as Szasz does, that the expression "mental illness" is a metaphor – has sparked enthusiasm among some practitioners, leading to what have been called anti-psychiatric currents, but among others it has aroused harsh condemnation, especially in the 1990s and 2000s. This condemnation has even affected politicians. President Bill Clinton claimed in 1999: "Mental illness can be accurately diagnosed and successfully treated as a physical disease." At the same time, his health advisor, Tipper Gore, declared: "One of the most widely believed and most damaging myths is that mental illness is not a physical disease. Nothing could be farther from the truth."

In fact, it is impossible to give a precise definition of mental illness, just as it is impossible in psychiatry to give a scientific definition of the standard or the norm. Nevertheless, a certain number of symptoms and behaviors are considered "abnormal" by society or bring suffering to individuals labeled with them, so much so that they can no longer accept their lives; can only accept them poorly; put themselves in danger; or have increasing problems interacting with their social group. In these cases, psychiatric intervention is legitimate and is unfortunately not always consented to by the individual with symptoms. Contrary to some anti-psychiatric positions, I don't consider that every intervention or hospitalization without consent is illegitimate or automatically tantamount to torture. But I respect this maximalist position because it does point out that in all cases, even the most serious, we must take into account a subject, a citizen endowed with rights and freedoms, who is suffering and speaking to us. Beyond cultural differences, there are invariants of behavior or modes of living that are considered abnormal found in all societies. Moreover, in one form or another, no society escapes confining individuals whose behavior deviates past a certain limit.

---

[28] Thomas Szasz, *The Myth of Mental Illness: Foundations of a Theory of Personal Conduct* (New York: Harper & Row, 1974). Szasz (1920-2012) was a clinical psychiatrist and professor of psychiatry at the State University of New York Upstate Medical University, where he spent most of his academic career.

Once we've established this general framework, we should point out that there are several ways to question the existence of a psychiatric illness – and we will see how matters stand for ADHD. The first and most radical way, which I've already mentioned, rests on the idea that every mental illness is a metaphor. Once one discovers a causal agent, as occurred with neurosyphilis, the disease is renamed. It leaves the field of mental illness and enters that of physical, organic diseases; hence the "metaphor" somehow becomes a "real" disease. The procedure provided by this example paradoxically delegitimizes the general tendency towards the a priori medicalization of mental illness, which, by definition, presumes a knowledge based on a hypothetical deduction rather than on sound scientific methods. It is assumptions like these that quite often leads to the consideration that psychiatric interventions have more to do with security guards and prison than they do with therapeutics.

Another mode of questioning and debate might be put this way: most "mental illnesses" are social constructions; they are born and disappear according to socio-cultural evolution. The most recent example, and a very convincing one at that, is the pathologizing of homosexuality, which was considered a mental disorder until the 1970s. Its disappearance from the classifications of so-called mental disorders was the result of a cultural evolution, a change in mores, progress in equality of conditions and a broadening of the field of liberties – *not* the result of any particular scientific breakthrough. Some "mental illnesses" are therefore only a reflection of the mentalities and moral limitations of a society, which makes their validity more than questionable.

Another form of questioning emphasizes the changing character of psychiatric symptoms. Hysteria, for instance, as it manifested itself in Charcot's day, at the end of the 19th century, was held to be a construction of modern phallocratic society, oppressing women and their access to sexual enjoyment. Psychiatric symptoms would seem to be related to the "discontents in civilization," and there would seem to be "fashions" or "fashionable" diseases. This is Allen Frances' idea, as articulated in his book *Saving Normal: An Insider's Revolt against Out-of-Control Psychiatric Diagnosis, DSM-5, Big Pharma, and the Medicalization of Ordinary Life* (2013). Similarly, depression, as mentioned, has been termed the disease of the century. On the other hand, it would never occur to anyone to dispute the existence of tuberculosis. Even if in some cases the social environment plays a role in the outbreak of this contagious disease, it exists outside its social setting.

The existence of a disease can also be questioned with technical, clinical and epistemological arguments, assuming that the expert consensus validating it is unsubstantiated and does not take into account important data, that it is more a matter of ideological bias or conflicts of interest than of a scientific approach. In addition, the existence of a symptom can be recognized without considering it as an element of a syndrome or a disease.

So, what about ADHD?

European psychiatric clinical schools, particularly German and French ones, have long recognized the existence of what they they've termed instability. For example, the famous German psychiatrist Kraepelin,[29] who was at the origin of the first classification of mental illnesses at the end of the 19th century, speaks of pathological instability. This type of instability manifests itself through behavior that is intolerable within its social milieu, is part of the pathologies and is often associated with delinquency, according to Kraepelin.

Instability in children was described as early as 1892 by the French School, with Boulanger and later Bourneville.[30] Then came the works of Alfred Binet, Henri Wallon, Georges Heuyer, as well as those of Jadwiga Abramson.[31] Psychoanalysts have since taken over from

---

[29] Emil Kraepelin (1856–1926) was a German psychiatrist who created an influential classification system for mental illness that served as a practical model for diagnosing and treating patients. He is also considered the founder of the field of psychopharmacology.

[30] In France, the emergence of the modern concept of ADHD comes from the notion of "mental instability" introduced in the 1890s under the leadership of the neurologist Désiré-Magloire Bourneville (1840–1909) at the Hospital Bicêtre in Paris, based on his observations of children and adolescents who had been labeled "abnormal." One of his students, Charles Boulanger (dates unknown), wrote his thesis on institutionalized adolescents and proposed a new category of patients, the "unstable," who exhibited normal intelligence but presented several clinical features that correspond to the current concept of ADHD.

[31] Alfred Binet (1857–1911) was an influential French psychologist who with his colleague, Théodore Simon, published the Binet-Simon Test, the first standardized scale of intelligence. The score on the scale would reveal a child's mental age allowing comparison with the norms of physical age. Henri Wallon (1879–1962) was a French psychologist and the founder of the field of genetic psychology, which views psychic development in terms of its formation and transformations from birth through adulthood. Georges Heuyer (1884–1977) was the director of child psychiatry at the clinic of child neuropsychiatry

them, for example Serge Lebovici, who with Roger Misès, introduced the concept of disharmony, and, more recently, Bernard Golse and Jean Bergès, who are working to find some meaning to this hyperkinetic disorder in order to contextualize it.[32]

But ADHD is not in the lineage nor in the posterity of these European schools. It's aligned with certain works from the English-speaking world that immediately considered hyperkinesia as a brain disease, as demonstrated by the various successive designations they gave it: first, minimal brain injury, and then, minimal brain dysfunction.

The history of ADHD begins in the 1930s, with Charles Bradley demonstrating that hyperactive children respond positively to Benzedrine, which is a psychostimulant. He wrongly deduced the organic origin of hyperactivity by a false reasoning that lumps together the chemical modifications brought about by the stimulant with the "repair of a chemical imbalance."

For about twenty years, hyperkinesia has been associated with attention and impulsivity disorders to constitute this ailment called ADHD, which is claimed to have a specific etiopathogeny[33] and to respond positively to psychostimulants. The DSM, since its third version, has implicitly endorsed this single perspective of organic disorder, clinical and psychoanalytical perspectives having been judged obsolete and hence totally ignored in the United States. This trend spread increasingly in Europe in the 1960s and 1970s, ever since the work of the Belgian physician Jean Demoor.[34] In the DSM-III of 1980, ADHD is designated by the acronym ADD-H or ADD, in other words Atten-

---

at the Paris Medical School. He was the first to introduce trained psychoanalysts in public hospitals. Jadwiga Abramson (1887-1944) was a neuropsychiatrist and the co-founder with Heuyer of the Clinic of Pediatric Neuro-Psychiatry in Paris and its director of child psychology.

[32] This brief historical description is inspired by an unpublished article by Bernard Gibello entitled *L'enfant agité*. Serge Lebovici (1915–2000) and Roger Misès (1924–2012) were French psychiatrists and psychoanalysts. Bernard Golse (1950-) is a child psychiatrist, psychoanalyst and professor of child and adolescent psychiatry at the University of Paris Descartes. Jean Bergès (1928–2004) was a neuropsychiatrist and psychoanalyst and member of the *Association lacanienne internationale*.

[33] Etiopathogeny refers to the cause and development of a disease or abnormal condition.

[34] Jean Demoor (1867–1941) was a physician and professor of physiology at the University of Brussels where he served as rector in 1911. He introduced the distinction between "educational retardation" and an "irregularity" of medical origin.

tion Deficit Disorder with or without hyperactivity. It would take seven years, during the revision of the DSM III–R, for the term ADHD to appear, translated into French as TDAH. The DSM-IV made no change but the DSM-5, published in May 2013, revised the data somewhat, lowering the thresholds for inclusion and introducing three modifications:

1. In the DSM-5 symptoms are no longer needed to conform to the child's developmental level whereas in the DSM-IV, symptoms were required to be more frequent and severe than those typically observed in individuals at a similar level of development.[35]

2. In the DSM-5, symptoms must begin before the age of 12, whereas in the DSM-IV the limit was set at seven years. However, with the 12-year threshold, it is possible still to label teenagers with ADHD who become spontaneously distracted and impulsive while still within the normal developmental range. It is the lowering of the inclusion threshold that may lead to a significant increase in prevalence: that is, the number of ADHD cases among the population appears to be greater, particularly among adolescents at risk of stimulant abuse.

3. For adults, DSM-5 reduces the number of symptoms required to diagnose ADHD from six to five.

ADHD therefore has a birth and history closely related to what might be called the American organicist perspective. It seems obvious, then, that all those who reject this solely organicist perspective are naturally led to reject the very notion of ADHD, which by no means leads them to ignore the symptom of hyperactivity or not to treat all patients presenting this symptom. For them, questioning the existence of ADHD stems from a methodological, epistemological bias that could be summarized as follows: to take a certain number of behavioral manifestations (fidgetiness, impulsiveness, inattention) as they emerge in the eyes of several observers as a diagnostic entity — and not just as symptoms — is less a scientific approach than a judgment of existence with, perhaps, a hidden assumption. To rely solely on the

---

[35] Child developmental stages are theoretical classifications that provide a general idea of normal change and growth. There is also a wide variation in what is considered normal. Therefore these categories are inherently uncertain and should be adopted in a flexible way.

fact that these behavioral manifestations exist according to the criteria adopted, to claim that they're an entity whose cause must be sought, in their eyes constitutes an epistemological bias, because once an entity is postulated, its cause must be sought. We can appreciate the circular reasoning involved: the behavioral manifestations that are very real in their existence (the symptoms exist and lead to a consultation) are isolated and assumed to be a pathological entity with their "cause" put forward as proof. And since there is a cause, there surely must be a manifestation. Supposed entity and alleged cause thereby mutually reinforce each other, as in mythical reasoning. In other words, it was right to isolate symptoms because there's a cause under investigation, and since there's a cause to be found, these isolated symptoms do indeed constitute a disease. In reality, the hidden assumption is that there exists an organic cause and it's therefore necessary to stick to overt symptoms. We are thus witnessing a clamping down of clinical research confined to physiopathology. For the moment, though, we find nothing convincing or conclusive here: perhaps it's the epistemological bias and not just a matter of time that's at issue.

There are also those who think that ADHD is the new "in" disease, because its symptomatic manifestations can fit into a sociological perspective. Indeed, in a society where autonomy is an important, if not the supreme value, as sociologist Alain Ehrenberg says,[36] ADHD is an obstacle to one's self-structuring, to adapting to the requirements of school life and to expected performance. Moreover, the multiplication of inducements by the various technological and communication devices has the capacity to stir up agitation, a permanent "zapping," incompatible with any sustained effort of concentration. The ADHD child would therefore be the child-symptom of contemporary society; the same would hold true for the adolescent and the adult. Or, as Yann Diener has quite rightly put it, paraphrasing Freud, "A child is being shaken up (*agité*)."[37]

But if we don't reject the idea of ADHD a priori, it's possible to challenge this disease with other arguments. For example, Richard

---

[36] Cited in "Épistémologie, sociologie, santé publique: tentative de clarification," *Neuropsychiatrie de l'enfance et de l'adolescence* 55, no. 8 (2007), 452. Quoted by Celine Clément in *Le TDA/H chez l'enfant et l'adolescent* (Brussels, De Boeck, 2013), 8.

[37] Yann Diener, *On agite un enfant: L'État, les psychothérapeutes et les psychotropes* (Paris: La Fabrique, 2011).

Saul points to no less than sixteen diseases or disorders responsible for ADHD symptoms, suggesting that in all cases a diagnosis of ADHD is a diagnostic error.[38] Among these sixteen "illnesses" we can cite vision problems, sleep problems, substance abuse, mood disorders, so-called gifted children, epilepsy, etc. Saul strongly supports the idea that the diagnosis of ADHD does not stand up to a clinical, neuropsychological, neurological examination, accompanied by complementary neuroimaging tests. It is not even a diagnosis by default, but rather by lack of time or of competence.[39]

Others, such as the authors of the collective *Rethinking ADHD*,[40] dispute the diagnosis of ADHD because, in their eyes, it isn't based on any sound scientific data. They believe that it is the result of the growing influence of different factors such as the pharmaceutical industry and parents' associations. By its nature, it also serves to mask social, educational, pedagogical and psychological problems. *Rethinking ADHD* takes stock of the available scientific data. Nearly ten years after its publication, the authors have updated their conclusions in some articles, but those conclusions remain unchanged in substance: ADHD has no scientific basis, it is a pseudo-disease.

The anti-ADHD challenge is also pursuing another line of attack: in the United States and Great Britain, there's been a major current of alarm at over-medicalization, especially in childhood, with its corollary, over-prescription. This trend was so alarming that as early as 2000, an article published in the online satirical magazine *The Onion* reported the misadventures of an American family: Nicholas and Beverly Serna and Caitlin, their four-year-old daughter. The description of this young child's behavior fits within the norm: she lives in her fantasies, her motor activities, her discoveries. But the article deliberately dramatized these behaviors and the child received the imaginary diagnosis of Youthful Tendency Disorder, described as a poorly understood neurological disease that will require treatment. The story goes on in this vein and the parents of this perfectly normal child say

---

[38] Richard Saul, *ADHD Does Not Exist: The Truth About Attention Deficit and Hyperactivity Disorder* (New York: HarperWave, 2014).

[39] And therefore, making the diagnosis could be viewed as a symptom of ADHD. [Translators' note]

[40] Vicki Anderson and Tim Godber, *Rethinking ADHD: Integrated Approaches to Helping Children at Home and at School* (Sydney: Allen & Unwin, 2003).

they are relieved to have a diagnosis. The cause has been found, so they're not responsible, they aren't bad parents. The article cites another similar case and, in conclusion, the parents of these perfectly normal children, having received an utterly unfounded diagnosis, say they envy parents who have normal children. This fictional story illustrates very well the opinion of those who denounce the aberration of medicalizing all childhood behaviors, losing sight of what a child is, its needs, demands, desires, and of lowering the thresholds for entry into alleged pathologies, prescribing unsuitable treatments with significant side effects and risking stigmatizing the child.[41]

Also around this period Christopher Lane alerted public opinion to the medicalization of emotions in his best-selling book *Shyness: How Normal Behavior Became a Sickness*.[42] More recently, at the time the DSM-5 was published in the United States, Allen Frances wrote an article in the *New York Post* entitled, "A Disease Called Childhood."[43] He took a very hard line with respect to the casualness with which American children are diagnosed with ADHD. In the United States, the number of children with ADHD has tripled in twenty years: it's a true epidemic. Allen Frances invokes a "triptych" of responsibility: any and all problems the child may have are considered a mental disorder, this disorder reveals a chemical disorder and this chemical disorder must be corrected by medication. In France, more and more voices are being raised against over-medicalization, over-diagnosis and over-prescription. This is notably the case of the collective "Initiative pour une clinique du sujet: STOP DSM" (Initiative for a clinic of the subject: Stop DSM), founded in the fall of 2010 by practicing clinicians including psychiatrists, psychologists and psychoanalysts. Given the current over-medicalization of children, ADHD has become of utmost concern, for reasons I'll explain when I discuss the usual approach that leads to an ADHD diagnosis. But, at the time of this writing, the Haute Autorité de Santé (HAS) [French National Health Authority] is

---

[41] "More U.S. Children Being Diagnosed with Youthful Tendency Disorder," *The Onion*, September 27, 2000, https://www.theonion.com/more-u-s-children-being-diagnosed-with-youthful-tenden-1819565754.

[42] Christopher Lane, *Shyness: How Normal Behavior Became a Sickness* (New Haven: Yale University Press, 2007).

[43] Allen Frances, "A Disease Called Childhood," *The New York Post*, March 31, 2013, https://nypost.com/2013/03/31/a-disease-called-childhood/

about to issue recommendations to general practitioners for ADHD screening.[44] We are waiting, without making any judgment, for what the HAS will say, but we hope that it will take most serious account of the remarks by those who present strong supporting arguments for denouncing the risks of over-medicalization. This risk is all the more recognized when we talk about prevention. Indeed, in medicine, it seems that we can reconsider the appropriateness of certain preventive examinations, like those for prostate tumors, that unnecessarily lead to invasive interventions and cause irreversible damage. Moreover, nothing is more uncertain, more risky, than prevention in psychiatry, especially in the case of children and adolescents.

The authors of the DSM-5 had considered including a risk of psychotic disorder among teenagers. In the absence of reliable data, they chose not to, yet the fact that they did contemplate it demonstrates the mindset of certain professionals who, in the name of prevention, might well bring on catastrophes. When you've worked with teenagers in the clinic, you know that in most cases predictive diagnosis is impossible: not every strange adolescent becomes schizophrenic. But instating a risk of psychotic disorder would surely have led to the expanded prescribing of neuroleptics for teenagers in the United States to avoid lawsuits since, if the young patient were to develop a psychosis later on, having withheld medication would likely risk liability for the psychiatrist. Hence, prescription coverage would have been standard practice for all teenagers behaving oddly, with the attendant metabolic side effects (excessive weight gain, diabetes, etc.) prevalent among the false positives. The same problem occurs with ADHD, not for psychotic risk but for drug abuse, addiction and antisocial behavior. Indeed, some professionals, drawing on dubious studies biased

---

[44] The HAS report came out shortly after the French version of this book was published. The report, *Trouble déficit de l'attention avec ou sans hyperactivité (TDAH): repérer la souffrance, accompagner l'enfant et la famille* concluded in part: "In the first instance, non-drug management must be implemented, combining psychological, educational and social measures according to the child's needs. If these measures are insufficient, drug treatment can be initiated. Methylphenidate is the only medication available to date and indicated for the pharmacological treatment of ADHD (trade names: Ritalin®, Concerta® and Quasym®). Subject to very strict prescription rules, it must be integrated into a personalized approach for each child, reassessed every month and prescribed in addition to non-drug therapy." [Translators' note]

See: https://www.has-sante.fr/jcms/c_2012647/fr/trouble-deficit-de-l-attention-avec-ou-sans-hyperactivite-tdah-reperer-la-souffrance-accompagner-l-enfant-et-la-famille.

by conflicts of interest, have spoken of a prognostic chain spanning from ADHD undiagnosed and untreated in childhood to problems of addiction, social integration or antisocial behavior in adulthood. I will be speaking again of this so-called prognostic chain that gathers new momentum when ADHD is extended to adults, since every adult with ADHD was once a child with ADHD.

Chapter 3: Diagnosis of ADHD

ADHD is one of the leading motives for consultation in neuropediatrics and child psychiatry. In most cases, parents don't seek consultation spontaneously, but on the advice of childhood professionals, individuals or associations that serve as a pre-diagnostic filter. They may be teachers who have heard of ADHD and who, in the face of a child's excessive psychomotor agitation or difficulty concentrating, talk to parents about ADHD. Sometimes they're friends or other parents who bring up this diagnosis; they may be instructors or coaches in recreational, sports or work centers or those centers' social workers; not to mention the clinical or school psychologists, general practitioners, psychiatrists or other specialists or specialized support networks for children with special needs, where they still exist.

We must emphasize the very important role of ADHD parent associations, which have easily accessible sites on the internet and offer not only reception services but also advice, guidance and support. These sites put out a vast amount of medical information and host discussion forums where parents can gather and exchange information.

In the best case scenario, the family is referred to a specialized hospital service where cases that don't seem to meet ADHD diagnostic criteria are not accepted. The fact that letters from parents requesting an examination or a consultation must be formatted to fit within the pre-established framework poses a serious problem, since it leads to a reciprocal legitimization of the supply and demand for care, a prescriptive shaping to suit the strict framework of medical discourse. Here there can be no question of what the psychology field usually means by a request, as the discourse is so reductionist. If it is right to denounce the therapeutic vagary, the obstacle course that so many families are undergoing, we must also denounce this formatting of the request, which aims to recruit "good" patients, who correspond as perfectly as possible to the treatment on offer. The formatted letters from families who want to be "recruited" by the care service are veritable application letters, and it's no exaggeration to say that they resemble CVs. Pre-diagnostic filters play a bit of a lawyer's role in bringing the "offender" into the legal discourse. In other words, on the one hand there are the "diagnostic vagrants," that is, those who take a long time to receive a diagnosis and appropriate treatment, and on the other hand, those who are left out by the medical formatting. The latter speak up less and testify more rarely on the internet, but that's no reason to forget them. In the "application" letters for a consultation at a specialized ADHD center, the families don't speak about their difficulties in subjective or personal terms, they merely give an overview of the child's behavior, a kind of recital of the signs of ADHD according to the DSM.

When the consultation takes place in the specialized center, the pretenses of the recruitment letter may fade away and the professional may listen to a particular request and a particular suffering – provided he or she is trained to do so, which is less and less the case.

The diagnosis of ADHD is generally made according to particular modalities, with the knowledge that there are sometimes important discrepancies from one reception site to another. It is based on the criteria of the DSM-5, which is the first source of diagnostic detection. As we have seen, the DSM-5 has lowered the thresholds for inclusion and its diagnostic technique contains numerous biases which affect both the professional who follows its recommendations and others who are involved in this technique: parents, teachers or special educators.

First of all, the diagnosis of ADHD is based on a survey of non-specific behavioral signs, such as hyperactivity or inattention, observed in multiple pathological conditions: mental deficiencies, epilepsy, intoxications, abuse, brain damage, significant anxiety, learning disabilities, problem family settings, giftedness in children or sheer immaturity. These signs appear for highly varied reasons out of a mix of biological and environmental origins.

In addition, we very often observe in children, over time and as they mature, a certain changeability of symptoms, occasionally interpreted as comorbidity. For instance, a child may at one moment present "defiant oppositional disorder" and at another "mood or anxiety disorders." This constitutes a serious confounding factor in randomized clinical trials because ADHD can be associated with signs that concern the emotional sphere, personality or communication. Differential diagnosis can be very tricky using the DSM-5 categories.

These behavioral signs have no pathognomonic[45] value, since they aren't pathological per se. All children are easily distracted, inattentive and restless. These signs vary from one individual to another, from one setting to another. There are tolerance thresholds and contextual effects, but a tolerance threshold is not a biological threshold. Consequently, what we measure are excesses. However, among these excesses, there is a wide variation in assessment and inclusion thresholds aren't objective. Tolerance to hyperactivity is probably not the same for a child who lives in the country in a large house and a child who lives in the city in a small apartment. Departures from the normal should not be confused with pathology.

In other words, even when looking for a detailed description and establishing a restrictive framework, the diagnosis of ADHD in the DSM-5 involves a large amount of randomness and subjectivity, both of which are considered biases according to the very principles of the manual.

With regard to attention as assessed in the DSM-5, it is appropriate to specify certain elements, admittedly a little technical, developed by Bernard Jumel in his very fine book, *Les Troubles de l'attention chez l'enfant* (2014). If we closely examine the DSM-5 diagnostic criteria for attention in ADHD and read the complementary literature to this approach as well as the comments made by the promoters of the DSM-5, three elements stand out:

1. For ADHD diagnosis, two lists of criteria obtain in the DSM-5, each entailing nine signs. In the list of "attention problems," difficulties or shortcomings in schoolwork are named four times, which suggests what we are seeking to determine or to identify. However with regard to the item "has difficulty organizing his/her work," it is not self-evident that difficulty in planning is necessarily due to an attention disorder. It should also be noted that the editors of the DSM-5 were careful to specify that this failure of organization must be distinguished from an oppositional type of disorder. In fact, it *is* an act of permanent and manifest opposition. But how and by what criteria do we distinguish between a failure of attention in schoolwork and a

---

[45] Of a sign or symptom that is specifically characteristic or indicative of a particular disease or condition.

dormant, episodic, intermittent opposition, etc.? In reality, with this approach the DSM-5 diagnoses "the inattention of the student who does not succeed in doing his homework alone" as "the inattention of the bad student."[46] These selected traits can be summed up as absent-mindedness and distraction, with a confusion between distraction and distractibility, which is the tendency to be distracted at the drop of a hat by any extraneous stimulus.

We know that distraction does not rule out concentration. A pedestrian concentrating on something may cross at a green light, being focused but distracted. Likewise, nothing is said in the diagnostic criteria about the *context* in which the child's disorders manifest themselves, or about the degree or nature of conflict that may accompany them. Here it is sufficient that they appear in two different places. The ADHD child of the DSM-5 is essentially an isolated child assessed according to his or her attention, *not a child in a relationship*, which makes it possible to assign him or her sole responsibility for this behavioral disorder. In conclusion, we can say with Bernard Jumel: "With the presentation of the nine criteria of inattention, by referring neither to what attention is nor to the conditions of attention, the only aspects of the behaviors retained have little to do with attention."[47] Rather, the DSM criteria identify what the classical clinic termed instability, whose triggering factors are multiple, highly influenced by their context, and which may range in variations of the normal as well as the pathological.

2. The DSM breaks with the tradition and methodology of psychological assessment. ADHD proponents generally assert that the diagnosis is clinical and that psychological testing is of no help. The questionnaires developed by the experts (such as the Conners Rating Scale)[48] characteristically list criteria that adhere to the DSM, but above all – with a few reservations – the test results are not meant to be examined within a dual relationship between clinician and child. However, this context of a dual relationship is very important in psychological evaluation, in psychometrics. Strictly speaking, the diagno-

---

[46] Op. cit.

[47] Op. cit.

[48] The Conners Rating Scale is a standardized questionnaire used to assess ADHD in children and adolescents aged 6 to 18 years old.

sis could conceivably be made without the clinician even having been in contact with the child.

Another more worrisome finding is that swings in attention over time and context, which all children experience, are put forward by the proponents of ADHD to discourage diagnosing the child with ADHD through individual testing. So if a child performs better on tests, concentrates better, is more attentive within some close relationship, this should not be taken into account according to the DSM. Barkley, one of the "founders" of ADHD, said that WISC III[49] – which is a model for psychological testing where a concentration factor (Freedom from Distractibility) saturates three of the tests – should not be taken into account, given the close relationship established between the child and the psychologist, even though that is obviously a clinical element of great importance which could shed new light on the disorder. In reality, a clinical psychologist or learning specialist experienced in psychological tests utilizing a WISC is much better able to say something relevant about a child's attention than these questionnaires that are closely based on the DSM (focused on behaviors alone and biased by subjective assessment) especially if these practitioners are trained in psychoanalysis and psychopathology, providing them with perspective and a certain depth of field. Attention has always been a problem for test theorists, and Version IV of WISC no longer has attention-testing examinations per se, but this is for the sake of scientific rigor, since no test, including the "cross-out test" specifically measures attention.[50]

In conclusion, the DSM-5 diagnostic method for ADHD resembles nothing so much as a power grab by a number of psychiatric experts wanting to justify their hypotheses, particularly those concerning supposed brain etiology.

---

[49] Wechsler Intelligence Scale for Children (WISC), 3rd edition.

[50] A cross-out test is done on a standard sized sheet of paper upon which everyday objects are drawn such as a shoe or a piece of candy as well as less gender-neutral objects such as a doll or a car. A teddy bear is also included, chosen for its "universal appeal regardless of the socio-familial context." Fifteen teddy bears are distributed over five columns, among 60 distractors (the other drawn objects) filling out the entire page. The examiner is placed in front of the child, and the instruction is given to cross out all the teddy bears. Before the age of three years old, the time of the test is not limited and is repeated until the child feels that it has completed the task. This test is used to evaluate visual attention and focus capabilities.

3. The last remark concerns the place of ADHD in the DSM-5, where it appears under the main heading of "attention deficit and disruptive behavior disorders," which manages somehow to bring ADHD and conduct disorder together under a shared label. This is overtly symptomatic, since neither the ICD-10 (WHO classification)[51] nor the CFTMEA (French classification)[52] does the same. For the ICD-10, ADHD is not in itself a conduct disorder and, for the CFTMEA, attention disorders without hyperkinesia fall within the broad category of cognitive and academic achievement disorders. Thus, it's not *attention* that seems to be the priority for the DSM, but rather the disturbances of conduct into which attention is classed.

The DSM-5 isn't the only tool used to make the diagnosis; but it remains the standard reference manual, and it is unlikely, actually unthinkable, that a diagnosis of ADHD would be made in a case that does not correspond to the DSM criteria.

There also exist neuropsychological tests that can serve as an aid in the child's overall assessment, as well as standardized tests, but none of these tests allows us to establish a diagnosis of ADHD: There is no standardized test intended to make an accurate diagnosis of ADHD. The various questionnaires or scales of measurement or observation can only be used to clarify the clinical picture of a child or adolescent. Standardized scales make it possible, for example, to determine the young person's level of difficulty adjusting to their social milieu by taking into account his or her chronological age, as recommended in the DSM-IV. But these questionnaires can in no way substitute for the doctor's diagnosis or the psychologist's clinical impression, which will be based on the analysis of a set of data. Nevertheless, judicious use of these measurement tools maintains its relevance within the assessment process.[53]

In addition to these evaluations in the form of tests, there is a purely medical evaluation (with a medical and psychiatric family history) where stress factors, the environment, diet, proposed medications and so forth are assessed. Furthermore, differential diagnoses are con-

---

[51] International Code of Disease of the World Health Organization, 10th version.

[52] Acronym for French Classification for Child and Adolescent Mental Disorders.

[53] "Le TDAH et l'usage de stimulants du système nerveux central" (Lignes directrices du Collège des médecins et de l'ordre des psychologues du Québec, Montréal, CMQ, 2001).

sidered, that is to say, all the pathologies that can be confused with ADHD such as anxiety disorders, visual disorders, learning disabilities like dyslexia and even autism. But what's essential and must be stated clearly is that diagnosis, strictly speaking, remains a clinical matter. Why is it so important to make a diagnosis? Some will answer that it's the traditional medical approach and that in the case of ADHD there's a chemical treatment. The diagnosis makes it possible to establish the indication for the treatment in an appropriate way. But I don't think that's the only reason.

Diagnosis in psychiatry has undergone a major evolution in recent decades. Thirty years ago, diagnosis was considered stigmatizing: practitioners were under-diagnosing and weren't obliged to give a diagnosis to patients or their families. Now, ever since the DSM-III appeared on the scene, psychiatric diagnosis has become "popularized," the general public has become increasingly aware of GAD, OCD, bipolar disorder and ADHD. This isn't a negative development, but those who thought that this "democratization of psychiatric diagnosis" was going to reduce the stigmatization of mental illness turned out to be overly optimistic. Today, psychiatric diagnosis has become a database entry: if you type into Google "obsessive compulsive disorder" or "ADHD," you get a multitude of articles, documents, addresses of associations bringing together patients with the same disorder, with opportunities for exchanges and forums. It's hard to sort through all this information.

Diagnosis, then, allows for a social link, which may have unexpected and contradictory consequences. For instance, in the case of school phobia, this may reinforce the subject's tendency to live in the virtual world, while in other cases, the social link may relieve the subject and help pierce his loneliness. The psychiatric diagnosis is an opening up of rights where the illness is persistent and leads to a condition of disability. These rights are more or less extensive, but they may represent significant financial, educational or pedagogical support, to the point that in the United States certain associations of parents of children diagnosed with Asperger's have lobbied intensely and persistently for the DSM-5 not to take Asperger's syndrome out of the category of "autistic spectrum disorder," so that they won't lose out on those burgeoning rights and allocation of benefits for their children.

In psychiatry, as in medicine more generally, it's not easy to announce a diagnosis. In some cases, the effect of the announcement can be traumatic at first, especially if the prognosis is considered severe; later on, the patient often represses its seriousness. In psychiatry, pronouncing a diagnosis varies greatly from one case to another. Advocates of ADHD willingly explain their interest in this diagnosis: it puts a halt to otherwise haphazard therapeutics; it relieves and puts words to suffering; it removes guilt, since the disorder is cerebral in origin; it may not confer a social identity but it does allow a certain social visibility. When I looked after mentally disabled children, I often heard parents blame doctors for not giving a diagnosis, meaning the diagnosis was implicitly "disturbed parent-child relationships," inducing a sense of guilt in the parents.

One hears psychoanalysts being blamed for making parents feel guilty, a matter about which I'd like to offer a few clarifications.

1. The question of parental guilt

First of all, whatever the diagnosis or the etiology of the disability, it is absolutely advisable not to make parents feel guilty in order to be able to listen to their sense of guilt and try to mobilize it, if only not to add to their suffering.

Parents always experience a feeling of guilt that crystallizes around several matters: "I didn't protect my child, I transmitted a defect to him or her in spite of myself," etc. It is the guilt of the progenitor. The mere fact of having given birth to a child unlike other children generates a feeling of guilt. It is important to respect this guilt as much as possible, without aggravating it, but also without fighting it directly because it is also the mark of parenthood, it is coextensive with the position of parents in general. There is no parenthood without a sense of guilt. It will be necessary to identify this sense of guilt, knowing that it can be projected, as parents try to make professionals feel guilty ("You're not doing the right thing..."), and this projection can lead to a break-up. One must therefore counteract this possibility by trying not to mirror this response. The professional is not an "ideal" parent, s/he must accept his or her limits. It's useful to make parents specify the inadequacies they see in the care and the support they receive in order to distinguish legitimate grievances from those that are imaginary or connected to an excessive desire for reparation.

There is no standardized response to parental guilt, but it may prove helpful to state that regardless of their level of disability, all children can learn, can enter into a learning process, and, whenever a new skill emerges in the child, it should be emphasized. Sometimes the sense of guilt is so strong or so unconscious in the parents that it can lead to a refusal of the disability, to a denial of reality, with accusations, not of incompetence or inadequacy, but of unfairness directed toward professionals. Moreover, the sense of guilt is sometimes linked to a desire for the child's death, which is hard to do anything with since it is virtually inadmissible, however conscious it may be.

2. The question of diagnosis

In general, a parent's sense of guilt abates when an etiology for the disability is found. This is why some parents go on a frantic quest for a diagnosis. Sometimes the doctors are the driving force behind this search, guided by the hope of a cure, or by someone claiming that if the doctor can't provide a diagnosis their presence is useless. There was a time when giving a diagnosis was discouraged because it was considered stigmatizing. Today, mindsets have changed. When someone refuses to diagnose autism, for example, they are seen as an incompetent professional who wastes time and thus an opportunity for the child, given the deeply-rooted idea that says "the sooner the better." Hence the legitimate anger of parents who've run into social indifference, inertia or incompetence.

The question gets complicated when the child suffers from an irreversible organic pathology. Parents have often appealed to many doctors in the hope of escaping the "verdict," but sooner or later the time comes for the diagnostic pronouncement. What is irreparable is always unbearable, and parents try to escape it. Faced with the irreparable, the professional psychiatrist, psychologist or psychoanalyst can play a positive role, *because there are always possibilities for change*, even very small ones, and it's necessary to convince parents to make use of them. It's not a question of full recovery or nothing; there can be strategies and techniques to compensate for a disability. The professional's role is to connect the possibility of change with opportunities for compensation, and to do this, one needs the parents' active support.

Caregivers must announce the disability or illness, and talk it over with parents: How did the diagnosis come about? Did the parents expect it? When did they discover or suspect the disability, if it wasn't obvious? What effect did the announcement have? It will be necessary to focus on the possible traumatic effects as well as to determine the logical time, the parents' psychic time, since these affect the acceptance of a care or rehabilitation strategy.

3. Phantasmatic representations

Whether healthy or disabled, every child falls within the phantasm of its parents.[54] For the child with a disability, the question of the phantasm is very important. Most of the time, the disabled child injures the parents' narcissism. He or she confronts them with an image that may evoke monstrosity, especially if the child presents major deformities. For example, this can put in check the desire for transmission of modes of behavior and cultural representations, diverting a parent's desired phantasmatic place for any offspring. This child will force a displacement onto the parents, of a psychic mobilization oftentimes very painful and which may require accompaniment, listening and propping up without encroaching on their role, their function. In certain support settings that are purely for the purpose of education (such as parental skills training which turns parents into educators), the family home must follow the same rules as the care or rehabilitation institution, for reasons of consistency. This can be justified within the framework of a language teaching method, but is out of the question when you're aiming to subjectivize the child, where ne-

---

[54] We have decided to translate "*handicapé*" with "disability" or "disabled" throughout the text to conform to acceptable usage in English. But the word handicap is still widely used in France. For a detailed study of what the word "handicap" signifies in French and how it is used, see Alain Giami, Jean-Louis Korpes, and Chantal Lavigne, "Representations, Metaphors and Meanings of the Term 'Handicap' in France," *Scandinavian Journal of Disability Research* 9, no. 34 (2007), 199-213. The American Psychological Association (APA) recommends using "disability" to refer to an attribute of a person and "handicap" to refer to the source of a disadvantage, which oftentimes is extrinsic to the person such as attitudinal, legal or architectural barriers. Concerning ADHD, this distinction is particularly relevant. Take for example the correlation between age differences of students in the same grade and the diagnosis of ADHD (which is elaborated later on in this chapter): a child in the same grade born in December is substantially younger than a child born in January of the same year and is much more likely to be diagnosed with ADHD. Such a child is not disabled but truly handicapped by the arbitrary starting date of the school year. The translators are also aware of the terminological debate taking place on the pros and cons of using *person-first* or *identity-first* language as in "person with a disability" or "a disabled person" respectively.

gotiating differences plays a decisive role. Otherwise, the place of the parents must be respected, unless there is a proven failure requiring a "placement order," in which case the parenting function is assumed by non-caregivers whose place must also be acknowledged. Generally speaking, though, the disabled child will have to confront the parental phantasmatic position, as the disability may compound the difficulty in overcoming the individuation-separation phase – which is often the case for children with Down's syndrome, where the child remains within the sphere of the parents' body. The caregiver's work may focus on this impossible or very painful separation that undermines the phantasmatic representation of the parents: as long as the child was not really born, he or she was not disabled. The phantasm makes it possible to compensate for the injury, and if this phantasm persists, the child exists for the parents more than for him or herself; he or she becomes a phantasmatic child who fills the parents' and especially the mother's lack. Any physical separation will be painful, because one does not easily separate from a phantasm. The imaginary axis is predominant, and over the disability there can also be superimposed a psychopathology of the child-parent interaction. The therapeutic work will then be to seek out ways to untangle these interactions.

Finally, it should be noted that the announcement of a diagnosis of schizophrenia or paranoia is always very risky. It can even provoke a worsening of the situation or a *passage-à-l'acte*.[55]

In conclusion, one can't be totally in favor of the diagnostic approach in psychiatry because it involves risks of objectification and stigmatization; but one cannot reject it completely because it may be useful to the clinician, and therefore to the patient. There may be no such thing as ethical psychiatric diagnostics, but there may be an ethical use of diagnosis in psychiatry.

---

[55] See footnote 8.

Chapter 4. The Scientific Basis for ADHD

It is essential to examine the arguments of ADHD's many defenders in detail. Some of them are driven by what could qualify as ideological choices. For example, in 2002, more than eighty researchers and clinicians from around the world became concerned about the poor media image of ADHD. Consequently, they signed a "consensus statement" stating that not to recognize this pathological entity would be tantamount to "declaring that the Earth is flat, the laws of gravity questionable and the periodic table of elements a fraud."[56] For them, not to recognize ADHD as a mental pathology is equivalent to reverting to an obscurantist, anti-scientific stance; but on what scientific arguments are they grounding their conviction with such certainty?

Within this group of researchers and experts are those who maintain that ADHD is *valid* as a diagnosis. In psychiatry, the *validity* of a diagnosis – what might be expressed as the possibility that a diagnosis covers some natural entity, like most medical diagnoses – is not contingent upon the discovery of an etiology, a causal agent. Diagnoses have demonstrated their validity long before an etiology has been discovered. For example, Down's syndrome was known and its validity recognized long before its cause was discovered: namely trisomy 21, an extra chromosome. Once the causal agent or etiology, or even the etiopathogenesis (that is, the mechanisms at work in the pathological process), is recognized, the validity of the diagnosis is no longer contested. Validity is based on the idea that the pathological entity it designates can be clearly distinguished from other diseases that resemble it in appearance, and that the same entity can be clearly distinguished from the norm.[57]

---

[56] Russell A. Barkley, International Consensus Statement on ADHD, January 2002, *Clinical Child and Family Psychology Review* 5, no. 2 (June, 2002), 89-111.

[57] There is a seminal article on the validity of psychiatric diagnoses: Robert Kendell

Even ADHD proponents are aware that this diagnosis has not yet been given an etiology; what we call "biological markers" have yet to appear. Yet, in the absence of evidence, a bundle of concurring assumptions is already in place. They include the belief that it is only a matter of time before biological markers (anatomical, cerebral, genetic or others) show up, so it would hardly be jumping the gun to consider that ADHD has a scientific basis. The problem, however, is that genetic studies aren't really conclusive. Whether they are studies concerning population, family or molecular genetics, they cannot prove anything other than genetic susceptibility, which is a very vague concept. In terms of neurobiological data, there's nothing decisive here either. It's true that cerebral alterations of the frontal and prefrontal regions, as well as other brain structures (for example the basal ganglia),[58] lead to symptoms of hyperactivity, inattention and additional symptoms such as anti-social behavior. But nothing specific has been identified here, only a semiological resemblance. When turning to the neuromediators, differences in the quantity of dopamine transporters (DAT[59]) at the level of the cerebral striatum have been observed,[60] but the existing studies are contradictory. In addition, it's hard not to cite the responsibility of methylphenidate treatment in these observed differences. Some have reported hypoactivation of certain brain regions in ADHD subjects; others note hyperactivation of other brain regions or still lower cerebral white matter volume in ADHD children who have not received psycho-stimulant treatment.[61] But ADHD is actually a complex set of behaviors, which may suggest that the search for a single neurological cause is too reductive.[62] Furthermore, the study sam-

---

and Assen Jablensky, "Distinguish between the Validity and Utility of Psychiatric Diagnoses," *Am. J. of Psychiatry* 160, no. 4 (2003), 4-22.

[58] Basal ganglia are a part of the brain that includes the thalamus and other closely related masses of grey matter. It is situated near the base of the brain and associated with the coordination and control of muscle movements.

[59] Also known as dopamine active transporters.

[60] The cerebral striatum is a cluster of neurons deep in the center of the brain and a principal part of the basal ganglia. It serves to facilitate a variety of voluntary movements.

[61] White matter is tissue in the brain composed of nerve fibers that connect nerve cells. The fibers are covered by myelin (a type of fat) which gives white matter its white color. Myelin speeds up the signals between the brain cells, enabling them to quickly send and receive messages.

[62] Angela Brassett Harknett, "Attention-Deficit/Hyperactivity Disorder: An Overview of the Etiology and a Review of the Literature According to the Correlates and Life Course

ples are too small and the diagnostic criteria are variable. It's possible that sustaining mild perinatal or postnatal brain damage may contribute to some cases of ADHD as well as to other psychiatric illnesses. There is also a collection of data on environmental factors, but these factors are extremely diverse: maternal alcoholism and smoking, emotional neglect, sexual abuse, mistreatment, food additives or coloring, etc. – factors which have nothing to do with each other!

If we make an exhaustive and honest survey of all the scientific literature and studies, what can we conclude? To date, the scientific data report that genetic susceptibility may be the most common factor in ADHD. However – and it's important to stress this – other psychosocial, biochemical and environmental interventions are also believed to be involved in the development of this disorder. In fact, what emerges from the current literature is that *no single hypothesis, no single factor, can adequately explain the development of ADHD in a child*. It may in fact be an accumulation of risk factors from multiple sources. In the end, we're not very far advanced. Therefore the position of some ADHD proponents obviously rests on quite flimsy scientific foundations.

ADHD proponents also have another approach, a neuropsychological one. Since it seems difficult or endlessly postponed to find a brain lesion or a chemical anomaly, some ADHD supporters have turned to functional hypotheses: there must be a functional neuropsychological origin to ADHD. There is no longer even the pretense of looking for a brain lesion or an imbalance in the functioning of neuromediators; it's only a matter of finding dysfunctions in the exercise of certain brain functions in ADHD subjects compared to a control group of normal subjects. These brain functions are attention, memory and what are called executive functions, that is, everything that aids in task planning, mental flexibility, adaptation, judgment, anticipation, the possibility of inhibiting certain responses and so on: a kind of "central computer" in our brain. Executive functions are particularly impaired in tasks that require an emotional charge or that may lead to a reward.

Dysfunctions in attention and short-term memory are found in children diagnosed with ADHD, but we must be cautious, as neuropsy-

---

Outcomes for Men and Women," *Clinical Psychology Review* 27, no. 4 (March 2007), 188-210.

chological tests must be very rigorous to eliminate all other possible causes of dysfunction, such as learning difficulties in reading or writing, visual problems, and so forth.

Several hypotheses and theoretical models have been used to support these neuropsychological findings, of which the three main ones are as follows:

1. Russell Barkley's theoretical model[63]

According to this theoretical model, attention deficits only originate from deficits in executive functions. This etiological theory is based on the hypothesis of an executive dysfunctional syndrome,[64] meaning a deficit in inhibiting or delaying a response or behavior. This deficit would be followed secondarily by a decrease in efficiency of at least four executive functions related to the frontal lobe:

–   self-regulation of the affect of motivation and alertness, which would be what allows the subject to separate facts from emotions
–   the working memory, which would allow, for example, linking together answers and reaching the goal
–   the inner language that calls upon internal representations to allow for control of behaviors (a notion which can join with psychoanalytical notions of symbolization)
–   the ability to divide up information and recombine units into a goal-oriented sequence of actions. It is this ability that would make the learning process possible

This theoretical model attempts to link behavioral and cognitive impairments, which is problematic from a methodological point of view. It can't, however, explain the subtype of the merely inatten-

---

[63] Russell Barkley, *Attention-Deficit Hyperactivity Disorder: A Handbook for Diagnosis and Treatment*, 4th edition (New York: Guilford Press, 2015). Barkley (1949-) is a clinical professor of psychiatry at Virginia Treatment Center for Children (VTCC). The Barkley model states that the basic problem of hyperactive children is a self-regulation deficit of affect, motivation and arousal leading to a behavioral inhibition deficit.

[64] Dysexecutive syndrome refers to executive dysfunctions in language, memory and calculation, and is associated with the frontal lobe of the brain, though other regions can also be affected.

tive, as its detractors emphasize. Different examinations (tests, tasks) apparently allow for analysis of the listed functions and validation of the model. But it doesn't validate ADHD, because many comorbidities may fit this cognitive profile. In addition, this model remains relatively simplistic, mixing operational,[65] linguistic and psychological functions, all in the name of an interpretation of behaviors.

2. Edmund Sonuga-Barke's delay aversion model[66]

In this equally simplistic model, it is no longer a question of inhibition but rather of *aversion* to delay or time extension.[67] This model postulates that ADHD subjects flee from any time delay. For example, the ADHD child, when faced with a choice between a small, immediate reward or a larger but more distant one, will choose the immediate reward, which is its way of fleeing any deferral. All disorders of the executive functions are viewed as consequence of this attitude toward time.

In this respect, I find Bernard Gibello's hypothesis much more heuristic:[68] "Unexpected and often misunderstood are the major difficulties they have in thinking and symbolizing time, chronologies, and durations. Their language makes poor use of the linguistic indices relating to time. Eponymous adverbs are used inappropriately; verbs are conjugated without regard for present, past or future tenses; the names of days, months, and seasons are learned and understood only

---

[65] The word "operational" describes the procedures by which something can be observed and measured. For example, the operational definition of anxiety may be described in terms of the results of a test score, the tendency to withdraw from certain situations, or the activation of the sympathetic nervous system.

[66] Edmund Sonuga-Barke (1962-) is a clinical professor at the Institute of Psychiatry, Psychology and Neuroscience, King's College London and deputy head of the Child Mental Health and Neurodevelopmental Disorders Theme at the NIHR Maudsley Biomedical Research Center.

[67] According to the delay aversion model, a patient diagnosed with ADHD would experience impulsivity — that is, a spontaneous and rapid response to a situation — without understanding the precipitating factors or the capacity to subjectively verify the validity of their response.

[68] The author uses the term "heuristic" many times. It refers to an approach to theory and practice that utilizes clinical experience, know-how and a broad-based knowledge derived from multiple fields of interest, and is opposed to the reductionist approaches criticized in the book. [Translators' note]

very slowly. But their difficulty in symbolizing time is not due to an insufficient vocabulary, but to a difficulty in thinking itself. It is hard for them to inscribe the present into remembrance of the past and anticipation of the future. I've given the name *dyschrony* to this disorder of time symbolization. For example, when examining twelve-year-old Alain, I find out that he can subtract two-digit numbers; I then make sure that he can state his age and that of his younger seven-year-old brother. My asking him, however, to tell me how old he was when his brother was born, plunges him into an abyss of reflection; he's unable to give the answer, though he seems to have the data for the problem and the arithmetic skill to deal with it. Systematic research has confirmed that the majority of unstable children in fact have the greatest difficulty thinking about time and chronologies."[69]

3. The model of Terje Sagvolden[70]

According to a Norwegian team, "waiting-time (delay) intolerance" is related to a dysfunction of dopaminergic mechanisms[71] involved in the phenomena of reinforcement and extinction.[72] The hyperactive child needs more immediate and repeated reinforcements than others. These hypotheses are correlated with functional brain scan images that provide a model to explain impulsiveness. There appears to be a dysfunction of the so-called "reward" system in ADHD subjects. But it's not at all surprising to find dysfunctions in hyper-

---

[69] Bernard Gibello, *Les Troubles de la pensée chez l'enfant instable: Dysharmonies cognitives, dyschronie et anomalies de la construction de l'espace de santé* (Papyrus, 2008), 243. Gibello (1932-) is a professor at the University of Paris-X-Nanterre and the director of the Laboratory for Cognitive-Intellectual Exploration, Child Psychology Clinic, at Pitié-Salpêtrière Hospital in Paris. He is the president of the French Psychiatric Association (AFP).

[70] Terje Sagvolden (1945–2011) was a Norwegian behavioral neuroscientist, a professor at the Universities of Oslo and Tromsø and adjunct professor at the University of Maryland in Baltimore.

[71] For an example of this perspective see: "Dopaminergic Mechanisms and Brain Reward," in ScienceDirect at: https://www.sciencedirect.com/science/article/abs/pii/S1044576505800387.

[72] In applied behavior analysis (ABA), extinction refers to the elimination of undesirable behaviors through the process of providing immediate reinforcement of positive behaviors while ignoring or refraining from reinforcing negative ones or using other disciplinary measures.

active children or to find that these dysfunctions are correlated with radiological brain imaging. Once again, we're given models and hypotheses without scientific proof.

Even so, ADHD proponents aren't represented only by scientistic reductionists. There are serious, respectable scientists among them, some of whom are basically saying that while we don't have scientific evidence to support the existence of ADHD and we cannot assert its validity, we nevertheless believe that the ADHD diagnosis is useful. We affirm its usefulness to advance research, for epidemiology[73] and for diagnosing hyperactive children. These scientists put forward the notion that diagnosis has allowed solutions to emerge for many families who were lost in a maze of medical-psychological consultations, tangles they saw slow down any medicinal solution to their child's problem. This is true for a certain number of them, due to a tenacious ethical or ideological resistance among psychoanalytically oriented clinicians to the diagnostic approach in general and above all to medicinal solutions for children. Yet the fact of constructing a diagnosis and promoting a disease with so little validity, especially concerning children, has led throughout the world to overdiagnosing and overprescribing. Furthermore, it has led to artificially inflating the number of ADHD children, a third of whom receive psychostimulants. Formerly, the problem was that the difficulty in detecting hyperactivity led to a delay in diagnosis, but now there is a very great problem of false epidemics, of false positives unduly stigmatized and treated long-term with psychostimulants.

So who benefits from the ADHD diagnosis? Clearly, certain families who have a hyperactive child in treatment, but especially the pharmaceutical industry, which peddles its products with aggressive marketing tactics. A pharmaceutical product needs a visible diagnosis, disease or syndrome. Thus ADHD has been a windfall for promoting methylphenidate, because in psychiatry, diseases are marketed and sold as common products. This phenomenon originated in the United States, but has spread all over the world. First of all, there is "disease mongering,"[74] which designates how the pharmaceutical industry introduces a new disease to "the market" in order to expand the direc-

---

[73] The branch of medicine which studies the causes, distribution and frequency of diseases in a defined population.

[74] English in the original. [Translators' note]

tions for use of a molecule it produces, or recycles some old molecule whose patent is about to expire thanks to a new marketing authorization. This strategy is very well described in *Le DSM roi, La Psychiatrie américaine et la fabrique des diagnostics* by Michel Minard,[75] but also in *La Fabrique des folies, De la psychanalyse au psychopharmarketing* by Mikkel Borch-Jacobsen.[76]

But marketing isn't simply done by pharmaceutical labs, whose job is, after all, to sell drugs: it is also done by mental health professionals. In the United States, professors of psychiatry or psychology[77] who've published numerous articles on ADHD have opened a site that looks more like a trade website than a medical one. They advertise their books or lectures on ADHD and offer online purchases of DVDs of their lectures, etc. When we listen to these lectures addressed to the general public, the communication strategy is always the same, with these specialists talking like preachers on behalf of ADHD. But it is their manner of self-presentation that is so remarkable, with most of them explaining that they had ADHD in childhood and/or that they have children with ADHD. This is a very shrewd communication argument, that breaks down many prejudices and barriers by confessing their own past ADHD or their descendants' ADHD, creating a climate of trust and availability on the part of the listeners. They've somehow managed to break down the caregiver/care-receiver barrier, which was the goal of the "anti-segregation revolutionaries" of institutional psychotherapy. However, the difference here is that this category of ADHD supporters doesn't rely on a political stance, but rather emphasizes a community of experience, of lived experience. They aren't just specialists in the disease, they know it from the inside, so they're close to those who suffer from it and to their families. Their confession proves that there is nothing to be ashamed of if you suffer from this disease, so it works against stigmatization. Moreover, because they're well dressed and radiate great social success, they're living proof that

---

[75] Michel Minard, *Le DSM roi, La Psychiatrie américaine et la fabrique des diagnostics* (Toulouse: Érès, 2013).

[76] Mikkel Borch-Jacobsen, *La Fabrique des folies, De la psychanalyse au psychopharmarketing* (Auxerre, France: Sciences Humaines, 2014).

[77] Two famous sites specializing in ADHD are those of Prof. Russell Barkley and Dr. Edward Hallowell. In France, this kind of quasi-commercial site, built essentially on self-promotion and promotion of ADHD, doesn't exist, and a good thing it doesn't!

you needn't despair over having a child with ADHD, that well-diag-
nosed and well-treated ADHD doesn't hinder academic success. Their
admission that they have children with ADHD, moreover, shows that
this can happen to anyone, that you shouldn't feel guilty if it happens
to you and that a genetic factor may be involved. These "preachers,"
or gurus, give lectures throughout the United States and in the English-speaking world. They work closely with parents' associations.
I'm unaware of any acknowledgment of possible conflicts of interest
with the pharmaceutical companies marketing ADHD products that
might involve them. But conflicts of interest often arise late in the
game, or perhaps not at all. In any case, these ADHD specialists have
a communication strategy in positive synergy with the pharmaceutical industries. Their argumentation sometimes mimics the advertising
leaflets published by the laboratories. Made-up like Hollywood stars,
they recite the guidelines like fine orators, issuing directives published
by the industry for health professionals but also for other stakeholders
such as teachers.

How should we view this global ADHD surge? With a lot of reservations, because we can clearly see the excesses and the abuses taking place in the countries where the surge has been in full swing over
the last decade. If everyone follows the example of the United States,
the Netherlands, Australia, the United Kingdom or Israel, we'll be
heading straight for a false epidemic because the diagnostic criteria of
the DSM-5 are insufficiently selective and likely to be abused by inex-
perienced professionals. Left to the observer's discretion, the DSM-5
criteria highlight non-specific behaviors found in the vast majority of
children in order to recommend appropriate chemical treatment. Add-
ing questionnaires such as that of Conners[78] doesn't change anything.
One remains at the level of a superficial and subjective appreciation.
Here is an excerpt from a questionnaire for parents:

*Below you will find statements describing children's behaviors
or problems they sometimes have. Read each statement carefully and
decide the degree to which your child has suffered from this problem*

---

[78] See footnote 48.

*in the past year by marking it with a cross in the appropriate column.
Each item should be rated as: never, occasionally, often, very often.*[79]
  - *touching or biting certain things (nails, hair, fingers, clothing)*
  - *insolent with grown-ups*
  - *has difficulty making and keeping friends*
  - *excitable, impulsive*
  - *wants to control everything*
  - *sucks or chews (thumb, clothes, blankets)*
  - *cries often or easily*
  - *feels attacked, is on the defensive*
  - *daydreams*
  - *has learning difficulties, etc.*

There is also formidable propaganda that is disseminated in the form of a discourse embodying the "good" that focuses on prevention, symptom relief and children's educational and professional futures. This is carried out by actors with very different motivations – be they honest and well-meaning, naïve and manipulated or predatory – converging toward the same point of view. Through their sheer numbers, intermittently exacerbated lobbying, medical activism and the new forms of "rationality" they supposedly embody,[80] they directly influence public health officials and decision makers in the field of mental health. As a result, those in power end up listening to a single discourse and no longer pay attention to other voices.

It surprises me, as a psychiatrist, to find that in France a number of colleagues have accused psychoanalysts of looking no further than their usual talking points, of paying no attention to the triumph of biological and behavioral psychiatry in the United States and all around the world. But these same colleagues express no interest in the consequences this so-called triumph has had for mental health in the United States – a triumph for the pharmaceutical industry and a disaster for mental health.

If we take stock of thirty years of dominance of the biomedical paradigm in psychiatry, ADHD is central to it, and its rampant epidemic makes some people say that we're facing a mental health catastro-

---

[79] Other qualifiers sometimes used are "not true at all, just a little true, petty much true, or very much true."

[80] In Chapter 8, we'll come back to this in connection with the concept of "neuromania."

phe. Psychiatrists cling to fads they share with some patients, and it's very hard for them to let go of these beliefs. But quite often evolution is taking place against them or in spite of them. My personal experience as a psychoanalyst has made me understand that psychoanalysis has been overestimated in its therapeutic capacities and its explanatory possibilities, but that it remains a formidable tool for listening and for subjectivation, and that it has many suggestions to offer in different mental pathologies. And so it would be unfortunate to throw the baby out with the bath water, and more and more psychoanalysts agree with this. But currently, rigidity and quasi-religious belief are to be found among the upholders of a biological psychiatry or a psychiatry acquiescent to the so-called scientific results of randomized clinical trials, the die-hard supporters of evidence-based medicine. They still have the upper hand, but not for long, because their dominance over the last thirty years has solved few problems and created or aggravated many others.

Chapter 5: The Hypotheses of Psychoanalysis

If psychoanalysts' theoretical hypotheses about hyperactivity are very diverse, they derive nonetheless from a shared foundation: they seek to interpret the psychological functioning of the child and its interaction with its environment. Psychoanalysts consider hyperactivity a symptom, not an illness. They relate this symptom to a broader framework, that of the psychic structure, or the psychopathological organization — neurosis, psychosis or borderline states — with the occasional aid of projective tests such as the TAT and the Rorschach.[81]

Most psychoanalysts don't recognize the syndromic[82] link between attention and hyperactivity for two essential reasons. The first is that attention is associated with hyperactivity to establish the diagnosis of ADHD, based on a purely neuropsychological conception of attention as a cognitive function. Connecting the two also refers to emotion, motivation, will and reward circuits. But for psychoanalysts, these are probably functions of the self, conceived as conscious functions, whereas attention involves unconscious elements. Instead, psychoanalysts speak of difficulties in the formulation and elaboration of thought as well as the possibilities of psychic representations.[83]

The second reason is that behind the conception of ADHD there is Gesell's theory,[84] according to which there is a parallelism

---

[81] The Thematic Apperception Test (TAT) is a projective psychological test developed during the 1930s by American psychologists Henry Murray and Christina Morgan. Proponents of the technique assert that the stories that assessed individuals make up about ambiguous pictures of people reveal or "project" their underlying motives and concerns and the framework through which they see the social world.

[82] Occurring as a syndrome or part of a syndrome which refers to a group or set of associated symptoms that consistently occur together.

[83] For Freud, psychic representations are the expression of the excitations of drives arising from within the body and entering the mind. [Translators' note]

[84] Arnold Gesell (1880-1961) was an American psychologist, pediatrician and founder and director of the Yale Clinic of Child Development (now known as the Yale Child Study Center). Gesell's influential Maturation Theory focused on the physical and mental de-

between the development of the motor function and that of the cognitive functions (attention, memory, learning and social behavior). Proceeding from this hypothesis, we can justifiably speak of *harmony* when these two developments are parallel and, when they're not, of *disharmony*, to use the term chosen by Roger Misès.[85] But this parallelism has given rise to the thought of deficit and organic lesion. When there is disharmony, the proponents of this theory don't see it as a rupture of synergy between motor and cognitive functions in which the environment might play a role, but view it necessarily as a lesional impairment that would help to explain the disorders in both the motor and cognitive spheres. We find the model for this approach in Von Economo's encephalitis,[86] described in 1919 during the Spanish flu pandemic, where there was no doubt about the presence of brain lesions accompanied by disturbances in the motor and cognitive spheres. But in certain cases, especially those involving hyperactivity where no lesions are found, it's assumed that there is one: this is the well-known *minimal brain dysfunction* or damage, or minimal brain lesion dysfunction. The reasoning can be formulated as follows: the brain lesion isn't visible, which doesn't mean simply that it doesn't exist – which is correct – but implies that it exists at a minimum. This existence at a minimum, which remains in the realm of hypothesis, is nonetheless presented as a dogma. This exclusive way of thinking oriented by organicism lies at the foundation of the conception of ADHD, and has turned its back on psychic reality to focus more and more exclusively on the cerebral and neurocognitive aspects.

Psychoanalysts have similarly rejected ADHD because it's too remote from their perception of and approach to symptoms. Indeed, the symptoms in ADHD are first and foremost mere behavioral signs, on the order of a fever or cough, by which doctors gauge and describe the intensity and temporary functional discomfort they occasion. Past a certain threshold, treatment is provided, which means in almost

---

velopment of children. According to Jean Bergès, Gesell was the first to speak of psychomotor parallelism. See: *Le Corps dans la neurologie et dans la psychanalyse* (Toulouse: Érès, 2001), 81.

[85] Roger Misès et al., *Classification des troubles mentaux de l'enfant et de l'adolescent* (Rennes, France: Presses de l'EHESP, 2010).

[86] Constantin Freiherr von Economo (1876–1931) was an Austrian psychiatrist and neurologist who is mostly known for his discovery of a rare form of encephalitis commonly known as "sleeping sickness."

half of the cases chemical treatment, with or without complementary measures. For psychoanalysts, hyperactivity, like any symptom, is part of a context and possesses a signification. But the signification of a symptom of hyperactivity shouldn't be understood in the same way as the meaning of a Freudian slip, a memory lapse or a dream. Hyperactivity has no meaning per se but only a general signification, indicative of the subject's psychic functioning in general. A major idea generally runs through all psychoanalytical explanations: that of intrapsychic conflicts. Every psychic or behavioral symptom is an attempt to endure or resolve some unbearable intrapsychic conflict. But the child or the subject who experiences an internal conflict also stands in relation to others. This means that psychoanalysts don't conceive of an isolated, solipsistic psyche. A subject's psyche is in permanent contact with and is constructed through others; the intrapsychic and the intersubjective are closely dependent on and interpenetrate each other.

One theory has long compared hyperactivity to a manic state. Indeed, the resemblance is striking from certain angles: flight of thought or impossibility of stabilizing a thought, agitation, psychic instability, denial of a given situation, etc. We also used to talk about hyperactivity as a manic defense. But this explanation was abandoned, notably by René Diatkine, who preferred to reserve this term for children who, apart from their instability, "don't distance themselves from strangers in a significant and repetitive way."[87] More precisely, "the manic defense must be reserved for another form of behavioral disorder, namely, overfamiliarity, an apparent absence of a minimum of angst or inhibition when meeting a stranger."[88] Yet the idea of hyperactivity as a mode of defense against depressive breakdown is not abandoned. Other authors refer to the child's difficulties using Winnicott's idea of the holding and containing environment, which corresponds to the entirety of care the mother gives the child to meet its specific physiological needs according to its own tactile, auditory and visual sensibilities, and its sensitivity to falling. It refers to care that adapts

---

[87] René Diatkine, Serge Lebovici, and Michel Soulé, *Traité de psychiatrie de l'enfant et de l'adolescent* (Paris: Presses Universitaires de France, 1997), 201. René Diatkine (1918–1997) was a French psychiatrist and psychoanalyst. In 1963 he helped establish the Centre Alfred-Binet, a psychoanalytic institution for children, and was an active member of the Société psychanalytique de Paris (Paris Psychoanalytic Society).

[88] René Diatkine, quoted by Maurice Berger in *L'Enfant instable* (Paris: Dunod, 2005).

to the child's physical and psychological changes.[89] The essential aspect of support, Winnicott emphasizes, is physically holding the child. The infant's center of gravity is not in its own body, but located between its body and the mother's. A lack of holding may occur as the result of inconsistencies on the part of the caregiver or educational ruptures – such as violence or educational forcing – or because of a depressive parental pathology, which is sometimes referred to as a psychic absence of the parents, of the mother in particular. The parents are present physically and yet the holding is insufficient because their preoccupations, their thoughts, don't primarily concern the child during the time of its care. This holding environment serves multiple functions in the child's development. It contributes notably to the psychic integration of the drives, to the development of autoeroticism, to the feeling of continuity of being and to the rhythmicity of basic functions.[90] Thus, failures of the holding environment as well as certain dispositions of the child can lead to a situation that manifests itself by hyperactivity.

For other psychoanalysts, the hypotheses would be that hyperactivity can be assimilated to a psychosomatic phenomenon, a serious somatic expression related to a disturbance in the formulation of thought called "operative thinking," with motricity compensating for this deficiency. Gérard Szwec[91] speaks of self-soothing processes in which calm is paradoxically sought through excitation, when the child finds itself unable to channel the excitement by means of bonding processes internal to the psyche. Hyperactivity is therefore not simply a motor discharge; it is a use of motor skills, a means of making intrapsychic connections.

Bernard Golse speaks of the fragility of the psychic envelopes at the root of a containing function of drive excitation. The notion of the psychic envelope has been described by many authors, including

---

[89] See: D.W. Winnicott, "Primary Maternal Preoccupation," in *Paediatrics to Psychoanalysis: Collected Papers* (London: Karnac, 1984 [1956]), 300-305.

[90] Rhythmicity is the presence or absence of a regular pattern for basic physical functions such as appetite, sleep and bowel movements.

[91] Gérard Szwec, "Les procédés autocalmants pour la recherche répétitive de l'excitation, Les galériens volontaires," *Revue française de psychosomatique* 4, no. 1 (1993), 27-51. Szwec (1947-2021) was a psychoanalyst, psychiatrist and supervisor at the Paris Psychoanalytical Society and the former medical director of the Leon Kreisler Child Psychosomatics Center.

Wilfred Bion, Esther Bick, Didier Anzieu, Didier Houzel and Geneviève Haag.[92] This metaphor designates not an object, but a function. The psychic envelope is born out of the contact with the object (the person in charge of the baby), which makes it possible to contain and modify the impulsive or destructive elements that the baby feels by transforming them little by little into thought.

The hyperactive child may therefore present a frailty of the psychic envelopes. And one could enlarge this notion of difficulties in symbolization of which Jérôme M. Forget speaks by drawing upon a psychoanalytical theory of motricity, which he calls the search for the *"decompleteness"* of the Other,[93] where what's at issue is the "symbolic inactivity" of the parents, to which "the "child's hyperactivity" is the response.[94]

Without claiming to be exhaustive, this overview of psychoanalytical approaches to hyperactivity suggests several general points. First of all, these theories are very elaborate, taking into account the

---

[92] Esther Bick (1902–1983) was a psychologist and child and adult psychoanalyst who co-founded the child and adolescent psychotherapy training program at the Tavistock Clinic in London in 1948 with John Bowlby. Didier Anzieu (1923–1999) was a French psychoanalyst and professor of clinical psychology at the University of Paris X-Nanterre and held other teaching posts. He introduced the concept of the skin ego as a mental representation of the experience of the body's surface. Didier Houzel (year of birth unknown) is a French child psychiatrist and psychoanalyst specializing in work with children. He is a professor of child and adolescent psychiatry at the University of Caen and head of the child psychiatry department at the University Hospital. He is also the author of numerous books and articles, a few of which are in English. Geneviève Haag (1933–) is a French psychiatrist and psychoanalyst who has developed psychoanalytic approaches to the treatment of autistic children. Wilfred Bion (1897–1979) was an influential English psychoanalyst and president of the British Psychoanalytical Society between 1962 and 1965. His many books and papers are readily available in English. For a good summary of the theoretical relationship between these authors see: Denis Mellier, "The Psychic Envelopes in Psychoanalytic Theories of Infancy," *Frontiers in Psychology* 5, no. 734 (July 15, 2014).

[93] "Decompleteness" is the state in which the child disengages from the experience of completeness with significant others which, when accomplished, allows for an unconscious representation of a loss to take place, which is fundamental to the subjectification process. When this process does not occur, the child has no place from which to speak or be heard *as a subject* and therefore remains locked into being the object of the whims of the parents (or significant others as representatives of the Other).

[94] Marika Bergès-Bounes and Jean-Marie Forget et al., *L'Enfant insupportable: Instabilité motrice, hyperkinésie et trouble du comportement* (Toulouse: Érès, 2010), 73. Jean-Marie Forget is a psychiatrist and a psychoanalyst working in Paris. He is the co-coordinator with Bergès-Bounes of the Paris School of Child Psychoanalysis and the collection "Psychanalyse et clinique" published by Érès.

child's entire psychic functioning as well as its interaction with the outside world. They differentiate problems according to the contexts, even micro-contexts, and to the psychopathological or structural organization of the subject. In addition, they're backed up by a much more qualitative than quantitative clinical approach, where transference intervenes: that is to say, the modalities of the relationship between the psychoanalyst and the subject and possibly his or her social environment. Obviously, they don't respond to the criteria of quantitative studies known as "randomized clinical studies," nor do they apply to all cases of hyperactivity, but they do open up therapeutic possibilities which aren't limited to psychotherapy of the child, the parents or the family.

Group therapeutic work for children, which is an application of the theory of the containing function, is an interesting illustration of how the group can play the role of a containing function. This work is all the more important since the difficulties of many hyperactive children are manifested in groups, particularly in the classroom group. In this diagnostic approach, questionnaires are increasingly relied upon that include a certain number of items concerning the child's relationships with peers. Therapeutic group work therefore responds well to the child's difficulties, but for psychoanalysts, it is not confined to work on behavior, however necessary this educational work may be. In a therapeutic group, the hyperactive child may either be a leader who is imitated, with the hyperactivity becoming contagious and the group uncontrollable, or the child may become an intruder who is rejected, with consequences for his or her self-esteem. It is therefore up to the adults to frame these spaces. The group is a libidinal experience, not an a priori given; it constructs itself and builds a "living-together." Adults have an educational function through the setting's structure, even if they don't use it specifically. The difference between the generations plays a containing function as an excitation-barrier. Adults aren't content with just observing, they propose mediations, activities, games that help to transform over-excitement into internal objects. These mediations can make it possible to transform what is often experienced by hyperactive children as a kind of chaos that disorganizes them and disrupts the class into a *story*, thanks to temporal markers and imposed suspensions. The group also helps the child to access the figurative. It may seem paradoxical to expose a hyperactive child to a group setting, when he or she presents difficulties in this type of situation. This, however, is the usual approach in therapy, the goal being to calm and then overcome them, even after a possible and undesired exacerbation of symptoms.

Professionals who have experience with therapeutic groups for hyperactive children note that there is often a phase where the group of children bond together against the adults. This phase of regression is very important because the dismissal of adults judged to be "totally useless" allows integration into the group, to the start of living together which is very effective, provided that the adults know how to tolerate this phase. We observe organized rebellion of the group, imitating a strike or a demonstration, with slogans often launched by hyperactive children. But after this rebellion, they enter a stage in which they must negotiate with the adults, speak with them: *this is interlocution*. As a result, the hyperactive child integrates and learns to be with others without monopolizing the presence of adults while also learning to bear being alone. As Marie Gilloots highlights, "The child is no longer the devil, unbearable and enigmatic. S/he is a child among others, and the family has gradually resumed its rights and responsibilities. This is perhaps the ultimate message that a successful group addresses to the hyperactive child: to make commonplace its presence in the recognition of its difference."[95] Group work isn't suitable for all hyperactive children, and not all groups are successful, but it is a valuable therapeutic asset in dealing with hyperactivity.

Psychoanalytically oriented professionals also use other therapeutic methods: relaxation, psychomotor therapy, psychoanalytic psychodrama and instrumental rehabilitation related to speech therapy, as hyperactivity is very often associated with instrumental disorders such as dyslexia, dyscalculia and dyspraxia.[96]

Some defenders of ADHD say that professionals – in particular psychoanalytically oriented child psychiatrists – are opposed in principle to prescription medication, and that as a result they waste a lot of these children's time, and further jeopardize their academic future,

---

[95] Marie Gilloots, *L'Hyperactivité infantile, Débats et enjeux* (Paris: Dunod, 2004). Gilloots is a child psychiatrist and head of the third sector (France's mental health services are divided into geographic areas determined by mean populations) of child psychiatry in the Hauts-de-Seine, Paris.

[96] Dyscalculia refers to an individual's difficulties learning basic math skills while dyspraxia refers to impairment in executing and coordinating motor skills. Dyslexia has entered popular discourse and concerns problems with reading.

failing to relieve the suffering of children who are often rejected, de-monized and lacking in self-esteem. While some of these reproach-es may not be unfounded, it's best to qualify them because, in over thirty years of my experience as a child psychiatrist, I've seen many situations of hyperactivity, including in emergency situations, caused by rejection or expulsion at school. In a considerable number of cases, we manage to calm the acute situation by taking the time to listen at length, to speak with the different participants. We can sometimes resolve such tragedies because there is often an imaginary component that overdramatizes the situation in both the participants and the in-stitutions. Resolution isn't always easy or feasible, either because of the intensity of the symptomatic manifestations, because a tolerance threshold has been exceeded, a combination of the two or for some other reason. It is then necessary to try a change of school environ-ment, coupled with very close support and care, when possible. If mat-ters don't improve or are exacerbated, recourse to medication should be prescribed, subject to a prior medical check-up. I've presented this situation somewhat schematically, but it does seem to me that psy-choanalytically oriented child psychiatrists generally share this point of view. Some colleagues believe, moreover, that prescribing methyl-phenidate allows psychotherapy to take place because of the relief it provides by allowing thoughts to be linked together. Nevertheless, the prescription of medication is only one aspect of the treatment and it should never be administered in isolation.

This opens up a corollary debate: ADHD proponents view the modes of involvement of the social group – parents, school or social setting – solely as reactions or responses to the symptomatic manifes-tations of the child. They believe that *only* the child should be treated, except in cases where the setting is very troubled and where the re-active character cannot be eliminated. These ADHD proponents em-phasize the need not to make the parents feel guilty, which is perfectly respectable. But the most pressing need is to treat the child, which in some cases requires mobilizing the parents beyond the educational process to adapt to the child's symptomatic manifestations. Truly in-depth psychic care must then be extended to the parents, and this approach has strictly nothing to do with guilty feelings. Sometimes it's the parents themselves who ask not only for help, but also for care. This process, however, goes beyond the scope of the "ADHD doc-trine," which remains a superficial and behavioral approach.

Prescription medication can be effective and sometimes quickly and completely reverses the child or adolescent's situation in a positive direction. Yet there are contradictory studies on the long-term effects of taking methylphenidate, some showing that this long-lasting prescription medication doesn't improve school performance or the child's future social situation in the long run. Others point out the cardiovascular risks and those related to height and weight growth. All these uncertainties justify a careful framework for prescribing it, as has been the case in France to date. But one of the major problems does not stem from dependency and its withdrawal effects, as is sometimes wrongly claimed. It is that *there are no valid criteria for determining when to stop this prescription*. For now, it is based on a combination of clinical judgment and the desire of the person taking the medication. Even if the withdrawal is sometimes successful, there are many cases in which it's continually delayed, which multiplies the risk of secondary side effects.

In my experience, most of the successful discontinuations of methylphenidate have come about because the subject felt capable and had good reasons to justify that confidence, such as a successful career, emotional commitment or a promising family life. This reminds me of the edifying testimonies of American or British patients organized in groups or associations called "survivors of psychiatry." They tell how, after being diagnosed, "labeled" as bipolar or schizophrenic, they took psychotropic drugs for decades, with disabling side effects such as obesity, extrapyramidal manifestations or metabolic disorders.[97] Then, they say, one day their lives shifted. Following some meeting or perhaps the launch of a project, they stopped the medication and are doing well, even much better. They now consider themselves to be *psychiatry survivors*. Of course, one shouldn't be completely taken in by this kind of narrative, where true and useful information is mixed with storytelling, the art of spinning a yarn that's well rooted in American culture. Nevertheless, these testimonies shouldn't be disregarded on the ground of their subjectivity. The current British psychiatric movement which calls itself "critical psychiatry" proposes a concept that allows for a better understanding of these testimonies. It speaks

---

[97] Extrapyramidal refers to the nerves involved with the activation and coordination of voluntary movements that descend from the cortex of the brain to the spine and are not part of the pyramidal system.

of a difference between "medical recovery" and "personal recovery." The goal of medical recovery is the disappearance of symptoms. And what's aimed at in ADHD is the disappearance of attention, hyperactivity and impulsivity disorders. This can be achieved quite quickly in some cases, thanks to taking methylphenidate, with the risk of premature demobilization of the family.[98] Let's not forget, though, that in the context of the ADHD mindset, which evokes supposed but unproven brain lesions or a chemical deficit supposed but not found, there is no way to speak about a return to the norm that could orient the prescriber toward stopping the treatment, the way you'd stop antibiotics after forty-eight hours of apyrexia.[99] Usually, a halt to taking methylphenidate is only initiated through successive testing or maybe a little bit of luck, or else, unfortunately, it may not even be contemplated.

However, if we move beyond this singular thought called biomedical, we can transpose the distinction between medical and personal healing. Personal healing would be defined as the state in which patients feel healed, released from their pathological state. They have turned the page, moved on to another moment in life and even if still suffering from symptoms, no longer experience them in the same way. This concept of "personal healing" speaks to me, and my experience with patients labeled ADHD who had been on medication for a long time confirms its value, however unclear it remains. The medication was a kind of "trajectory stabilizer" for them, but at the same time, they benefited from the work of psychotherapy. It is that work which allowed them to achieve personal healing. Analytical psychotherapy, sometimes referred to as analytically inspired psychotherapy, is very effective in the long term for those who can or wish to undertake it, both adolescents and adults.

Behavioral techniques also have their usefulness, but they remain anchored to the behavioral level, without concern for the psychic life, even though they can sometimes be practiced by professionals who take psychic life into account.

---

[98] Demobilization usually refers to a nation's army standing down from combat-ready status, either due to victory in war or because a crisis has been peacefully resolved and military force is no longer necessary. An apt analogy here. [Translators' note]

[99] In pathology, apyrexia is the normal interval or period of let-up in a fever. It can also refer to the absence of a fever.

At all stages – diagnosis, evaluation, implementing treatment, follow-up and termination – it's necessary to keep an open mind, without preconceptions, combining methodological caution with the search for the best solution. It's necessary to take into account research data in the neurocognitive field, but also to broaden the perspective by drawing on data concerning the subject in his or her mutual relationship to his or her family, school and social environment, with both diachronic and synchronic perspectives simultaneously in mind.

Chapter 6: New Therapeutic Methods

Earlier, I pointed out that I find very little diagnostic validity underlying ADHD. It is a manifestation of superficial descriptive behavioral psychiatry that finds its justification in the success achieved by the chemical molecule methylphenidate in the context of instability and attention disorders. The neurocognitive theories that support ADHD are mere hypotheses about cognitive functions, but are in no way proof of the existence of ADHD. While it is essential to take advances in neuroscience into account, we must be aware that their current contribution is very problematic for the everyday psychiatric practice of professionals confronted with hyperactive children.

Indeed, in more than a third of cases, the child designated as having ADHD suffers from learning disabilities (difficulties in reading, writing, mathematics) and is subjected to neuropsychological explorations that gear investigations toward a search for disorders of executive functions including organization, work planning, cognitive flexibility as well as memory, social interaction, visual and auditory selective attention, divided attention or sustained attention, inhibition processes and their defects, and more.[100] The test results confirm lower performance than would be expected from a child of this age and specify the subject's areas of ability. And since these children present the behavioral picture that includes ADHD, it is sometimes inferred, through false reasoning, that real cognitive difficulties are the cause of this behavioral picture and therefore, that ADHD exists.

In fact, in the subjects included in the behavioral picture designated as ADHD, cognitive difficulties are quite diverse and not specific to ADHD. There is no typical or standard cognitive profile associated

---

[100] See for example: Joni Holmes et al., "The Diagnostic Utility of Executive Function Assessments in the Identification of ADHD in Children," *Child and Adolescent Mental Health* 15 (2010), 37-43, https://doi.org/10.1111/j.1475-3588.2009.00536.x. [Translators' note]

with ADHD. However, observed cognitive difficulties call for therapeutic response modalities that aim to reduce them. This results in a very long series of recommendations to parents and teachers, as well as devices all modeled on the behavioral method, with positive and negative behavioral reinforcements in addition to measures derived from everyday psychology, common sense and even technological aids. Interventions will be implemented to reduce distractions related to ADHD in the classroom such as recommendations to put plastic tips under the legs of chairs and tables in order to reduce noise pollution and distraction caused by noise; suggestions that the ADHD child use headphones or work in an isolated corner; giving permission for them to get up and move around in the classroom; and placing a therapy ball in the child's chair to allow the child to move around freely when concentrating. Furthermore, the teacher will be given suggestions to establish clear and stable routines, schedule announcements or transitions, give the child with ADHD clear orders, allow the child to answer the teacher's questions first and place the child somewhere in the classroom that offers the best area for participation. The child who behaves well is rewarded, and the ones who do not are reprimanded.

In addition to this, more ambitious programs have been developed to promote social integration, social skills training and (more enigmatically) to strengthen the concept of self. Neurocognitive assessments can also lead to cognitive remediation-type treatments, where weekly or more frequent sessions aim to help the subject to overcome cognitive deficits related to memory or attention, with the support of specialized and playful software adapted to children. Parents are also targets of psycho-educational programs. The justification for these "parenting skills training programs" of which Barkley's parent training program (PTP) is the prototype, is indisputable.[101] Parents with hyperactive children suffer, and this suffering must be taken into account. Here's how the promoters of the PTP justify it: "The analysis of the environment and family dynamics in the context of ADHD leads us to three major observations. First of all, it seems undeniable that ADHD damages family relationships at all levels, especially parent-child relationships. Second, inappropriate parenting practices seem to play

---

[101] See for example: William Pelham Jr. and Gregory Fabiano, "Evidence-Based Psycho-Social Treatments for Attention-Deficit/Hyperactivity Disorder," *Journal of Clinical Child & Adolescent Psychology* 37, no. 1 (2008), 184-214.

a determining role in the development and maintenance of children's maladaptive behaviors in the short, medium and long term. Finally, it is essential to take into consideration the degree of parental distress as well as parental cognitions, given their repercussions both in the quality of life of parents and children and in the adoption of inappropriate educational practices. These three findings justify the relevance of parenting skills training programs in the context of ADHD."[102] It is an ambitious program, and the detailed study of all these educational, psycho-educational and rehabilitative measures calls for several remarks.

A child burdened with the presumed diagnosis of ADHD is considered, above all else, a "child with a disability." Their condition, therefore, might not ever rise to the level of a pathological disease but will remain solely within the sphere of the "disability." From this perspective, the goal of the treatment becomes overcoming the disability or erasing it as much as possible. This is done through ever more sophisticated means but whose objectives are adapting the child's behaviors to social and family norms and not a matter of psychological care. This goal is moreover clearly stated with regard to PTPs: consequently, the general objective of PTPs is to set up a family dynamic that suitably motivates the child to behave appropriately according to the rules laid down by the parents. It is clear that the aim of this method is to increase children's obedience to the parents' rules and demands. The same goes for the rules at school, which prompts me to reiterate what many others have said before me: ADHD is "the disease of disruptive children," children who upset school and family life through their behavior. It may seem out of place to criticize an action that aims at restoring a certain family harmony, but my criticism is not directed at this noble goal.

I agree with those who've rejected this rigid pathology/disability separation. They stress the fact that mental pathologies sometimes lead to severe disabilities and that, conversely, the persistence of disadvantages in social interactions can contribute to the fixation of quite constraining psychopathological mechanisms. Thus, when-

---

[102] Celine Clément, op. cit., 121. Clément is Professor of Psychology and Educational Sciences at the University of Strasbourg in France where she serves as the scientific manager of the "Barkley program," which provides parental guidance training for parents of children with behavioral problems.

ever they can, caregivers must promote a convergence and positive synergy between structural changes in psychic organization and the progress made in the field of school, family or later social adaptation. In practice, some advocates of rehabilitation methods are open to a joint approach, consisting of multidimensional interventions affecting the cognitive and psychic sphere. However, the directives intended for professionals, the books intended for the public and even those targeted to the general public are mostly silent on these multidimensional interventions or they are relegated to the background. These documents give the impression of a solid theory with a very wide field of application advancing scientifically-founded conduct to be followed. However, that is misleading. The focus on the disability has consequences at several levels. Firstly, the recognition of a disability by a medical authority can open up rights, in the form of various types of aid and allowances, which doesn't in itself warrant criticism. Quite the contrary: society has a duty to show solidarity with families affected by disability, particularly mental disability. But this opening up of rights may generate some perverse effects.

In addition, most of the programs offered cannot be put into concrete practice under standard school conditions. They require adult mobilization around the child, which is conceivable only in small class sizes or with the help of almost full-time school assistants. When you consider that in the United States, there are some states with more than 15 percent of children between the ages of 7 and 17 labeled with ADHD, these programs are outright impossible to implement. Moreover, the promoters of these programs readily acknowledge that their results can't be generalized and that their studies were conducted under non-standard school conditions.

Having worked for many years in medical-pedagogical and medical-professional institutes that received children with psychiatric difficulties and developmental disorders, I believe that most of the pedagogical and educational recommendations advocated by ADHD proponents are, in fact, already being implemented mainly in the specialized classes or workshops of these institutions. However, they're being applied without a behavioral theory to guide the actions of teachers and special educators. Most of them mix references, from psychoanalysis to behaviorism, combined with a good deal of pragmatism, which has the significant advantage of leaving their practices open and flexible, even if the evaluation of children's evolution is less systematized and less quantified. We could say that such evaluations are only *apparently* more subjective, because the typical evaluation or self-evaluation questionnaires used in other settings are far from free of a subjective dimension. But this dimension is covered up, masked by a number, an algorithm, a graph or a scale – by measurable data. Here again, the measurable and the subjective should not be systematically opposed. In psychiatry, for instance, when we listen to patients talk about their affects, moods or desire to commit suicide, we take into account both the subjective self-evaluation – the evaluation that they make of their own condition – and the subjective hetero-evaluation that we make according to what we hear, the degree of denial or possible provocation that the patient presents. And our experience allows us to arrive at a kind of measure of seriousness that leads us possibly to orient the therapeutic action in a certain direction.

Finally, I wonder what may be the effects of these parenting skills training and cognitive remedial aid programs? Do they work? And when they work, is it for the scientific reasons categorically stated by their promoters? Based on my own experience and by reading the clinical vignettes of the authors who practice these methods, I definitely don't think so. As a practitioner oriented by psychoanalysis, I receive families to whom these methods have been proposed and who have been dissatisfied with them. Without a doubt this is a non-representative sampling, but when these families speak about the failures these methods embody, one can conversely gain understanding for the reasons these same methods are successful elsewhere. I will offer a few suggestions: there are people who are resistant to psychological investigation and who are sensitive to the "scientific" environment surrounding these methods. These people may react positively to a regressive "school" framework where you "learn" to become a parent and where you're told what to say or do. For these parents, such a framework is reassuring, it makes them feel less guilty and it allows them to put aside more personal issues. Successive evaluations make it possible to measure progress and have a positive impact on their self-esteem and narcissism which are supported by the therapeutic alliance, the placebo effect and adherence to the method as well as anticipation of the outcome. As for the children, they receive much more than technical or technological help in cognitive remediation. We must also take into account the appreciation children can have for the support and special attention they're given, as well as their possible wish to please the adult, among other comparable responses.

If ADHD represents a disability, with the stigmatizing effects that this can have, it seems all the more imperative that it be given the most valid and sensitive definition possible. A clear line needs to be drawn between ADHD and variations from the normal, with another line drawn between ADHD and other psychiatric diagnoses. This isn't in fact the case, because all diagnostic devices, such as the DSM-5, are *dimensional*. The dimensional is a kind of gradient where we go from normal to its variations and then to the pathological. We could illustrate this with the example of temperature: 98.6°F is the norm; 97.5°F to 98.9°F are the variations of the norm; beyond 98.9°F, we're speaking of fever. Everyone has fluctuations in attention, especially so-called "bad" or unmotivated students, and the variations from the normal are in the same dimension as pathologies of attention. Because it's a question of frequency and degree, a consensual decision determines what degree on this dimensional axis signifies entry into the pathological. The DSM-5 states that the diagnosis of ADHD is made if the subject presents six or more inattentive behaviors out of a list of nine for a period of at least six months. These behaviors must result in a proven functional impairment in school, university or professional work; they must be incompatible with the child's level of development; they must be present in two different types of settings (family, school, etc.), and furthermore, not be better explained by other diagnoses such as anxiety disorder, dissociative disorder, etc. Here are a few examples of behaviors: "often has difficulty sustaining attention at work or at play," "often seems not to be listening when spoken to personally," "often has difficulty organizing work or activities." In these statements, the dimensional character is perfectly visible, underlined by the repetition of the word "often." What does "often" mean? How can it be measured? It's apparent that we're entirely within the dimensional with respect to the diagnosis of ADHD. Of course, it's not just in psychiatry that we find diagnoses based on the dimensional register, but the combination of dimensional character without any scientifically valid reference points poses a real problem.

The dimensional is opposed to the categorical, the latter referring to categories, entities and clearly delineated structures that are quite distinct from one another, such as typhoid fever and tetanus. The DSM-5 and ADHD proponents consider ADHD to be a neatly defined diagnostic category. However, it is the success of a chemical treatment that has perpetuated this ADHD category.

In my view, ADHD doesn't constitute a valid category in so far as the factors of diagnostic confusion are major and numerous. It is crucial to examine in detail a few telling and striking examples of these confounding diagnostic factors that lead to a false epidemic, false positives and over-medication, especially for children who need none.

Psychological immaturity is the first confounding factor I'll mention here. While it may be difficult to define according to scientific criteria, there is an objective benchmark: age. Children born at the beginning of January often find themselves in the same class as those born at the end of December of the same year. Therefore, there is almost a year's difference between them. A study of 900,000 early elementary school children in British Columbia showed that a male child born in December, and therefore substantially younger than his classmates, was 30 percent more likely to be diagnosed with ADHD than a male child born in January. For girls, the difference was as high as 70 percent. The fate for determining ADHD chemical treatment also varied: boys born in December were 41 percent more likely to receive pharmacological treatment than their January-born peers. December-born girls, who are therefore the youngest in their classes, were 77 percent more likely to be methylphenidate-mediated than their peers born in January.[103] The authors of the study conclude that immaturity is an important cause of diagnostic confusion, that it can induce behavioral patterns similar to ADHD and become an important cause of over-diagnosis as well as over-prescription. Consequently, they caution practitioners to be very careful about this confounding factor.

The second factor that seriously challenges the validity and soundness of the ADHD diagnosis concerns those who are referred to as intellectually precocious children, formerly known as "gifted." The existence of this category is much debated and quite problematic in many ways, but it is an issue of increasing importance since some studies have shown that these children are falsely diagnosed with ADHD. The idea developed by the flagship study on this problem

---

[103] Richard L. Morrow et al. "Influence of Relative Age on Diagnosis and Treatment of Attention-Deficit/Hyperactivity Disorder in Children," *Canadian Medical Association Journal* 184, no. 7 (April 17, 2012), 755-762.

is that so-called gifted children are not reducible to children with an IQ above 130.[104] These children have a heterogeneous cognitive profile with areas of very great strength as well as weaknesses, which can lead to difficulties or even failure at school. In addition, they are children who present a certain number of psychological characteristics and particular character traits such as a particular attachment to truth and justice, a keen sense of observation, very great intellectual curiosity and quick comprehension. They are creative, inventive, perceptive with respect to cause and effect relationship, and have a very good language level. These children are also apt to have negative traits such as being too critical of others, too attached to details, bossy, etc. which often leads to diagnoses of ADHD. What are we to think of this description?

I don't know if this concept of intellectually precocious children is valid, but it's very interesting for several reasons. First of all, it shows that the ADHD picture may be the result of complex phenomena, some of which are wrongly considered pathological. Indeed, it is important in a democratic society to differentiate between mental pathologies and original or minority ways of being. I don't agree with including all subjects whose behavior is out of the norm within mental pathology. It's not surprising that children whose way of thinking and intelligence aren't adapted to the school system find themselves in difficulty. And the succession of misunderstandings and mutual rejections that may ensue can lead to the expression of a behavioral picture often linked with ADHD. But focusing on these children's behavior places them, once again, at the center of the problem – not at the center of concern but at the center of the problem – and spares the scholastic institution, and its educational and pedagogical policies, from taking responsibility. Thus, there is an advantage to considering the category of intellectually precocious children regardless of its vagueness. In the United States, a study shows that the number of children with ADHD is increasing in schools with a higher level of requirements than is average in other schools. The functioning of the educational institution is therefore not neutral. Moreover, psychiatry should not be put in the service of eroding differences, nor should it stand in the way of developing potentialities, especially in children. The normal-

---

[104] See: https://www.sengifted.org.

ization of behaviors, while necessary at times, also has its limits. Some authors rely on studies to claim that intellectually precocious children no longer present a behavioral picture of ADHD when they are in a school environment that is adapted to them.[105] However, it seems that the studies in question suffer from bias, given the difficulty in agreeing on the definition of intellectually precocious children. Clearly, this leads to a real problem if one wants to establish and compare samples, as Nicolas Gauvrit points out very well in *Les Surdoués ordinaires*.[106]

There are many other confounding factors, such as anxiety (called "anxiety disorder" in DSM-speak), epilepsy, sleep disorders, oppositional behaviors and all restless reactions to family, social, educational dysfunctions and so on, that falsely lead to an apparent diagnosis of ADHD. But these confounding factors stem more from medical practice and differential diagnosis and are thus less significant than the examples of immaturity and precocious intelligence for objecting to the paradigms that the DSM method uses to promote ADHD as a disease. These paradigms are strictly medical-biological with a component of behavioralism thrown in. Notwithstanding, and perhaps unbeknownst to those who are its vectors, they reflect a certain vision of the child, considered disruptive because of his or her brain dysfunctions, whose behaviors must be normalized, and above all, increasingly, targeted by medication. In *Childhood Under Siege: How Big Business Targets Your Children*,[107] Joël Bakan speaks out against the reduction of the child to a consumer. First among the products he identifies as being consumed are psychiatric drugs, which are called "psychotropics." This problem deserves a very close examination in the case of ADHD.

---

[105] Kelly Henderson, "Teaching Children with Attention Deficit Hyperactivity Disorder: Instructional Strategies and Practices," U.S. Department of Education (2008); Peter Blatchford, Anthony Russell et al., "The Effect of Class Size on the Teaching of Pupils Aged 7-11 Years," *School Effectiveness and School Improvement* 18, no. 2 (2007); Peter Blatchford, Kam Wing Chan et al., eds., *Class size: Eastern and Western Perspectives* (London-New York: Routledge, 2016); Geraldina Gaastra, Yvonne Groen et al., "The Effects of Classroom Interventions on Off-Task and Disruptive Classroom Behavior in Children with Symptoms of Attention Deficit/ Hyperactivity Disorder: A Meta- Analytic Review," *PLOS ONE* 11, no. 2 (2016).

[106] Nicolas Gauvrit, *Les Surdoués ordinaires* (Paris: PUF, 2014). Gauvrit is a lecturer in the cognitive sciences at the École pratique des hautes études in Paris.

[107] Joël Bakan, *Childhood Under Siege: How Big Business Targets Your Children* (New York: Free Press, 2012).

Chapter 7: Psycho-marketing and Big Pharma

In the last three decades, the use of ADHD medication has exploded in most Western countries. In the United States, consumption has increased twenty-fold during this period, and other countries in the West are following consumption curves in the same direction, albeit at a slower pace. In this context, it is important to note that the United States has a characteristic found nowhere else except in New Zealand: pharmaceutical companies can address consumers directly. In those countries, it is possible to see advertisements for drugs on television channels, for example, vignettes in which an actor emphasizes symptoms that may be almost ordinary affects or behaviors to which we don't necessarily pay much attention. The commercial suggests that the "disease" one suffers from is often unknown, that while it may go unnoticed, it is much more widespread than one thinks. Then a voice-over explains that there is a cure: the very medicine that is being promoted! It's interesting to analyze the mechanisms behind such sketches: advertisers play above all on identification with the actor, on the angst everyone feels, on the general frailty of the human condition and in particular, on our psychical equilibrium. They try to prompt doubt about our own health or at least a questioning of it – for what, after all, is being human if not a high-risk condition? Suggestion as contagion can play a role in convincing someone that they suffer from a disease, or at least in driving them to consult a specialist, especially if the disease isn't clearly set apart from variations on the normal. Sometimes a well-known movie or television actor is featured, or even a public figure who accompanies his or her performance with a confession: they have actually been diagnosed with a mental illness, and this particular cure has relieved them.

The impact of these constructed scenarios and confessions on the broader public's experience is far from negligible. Ads of this type exist for ADHD and its medications. But, in this case, an additional mechanism is at work: without being too explicit, they must rouse parents' anxiety and their feelings of guilt regarding their protective role. In the end, the solution is staring them in the face: the medication. Sometimes it's not mentioned at all, or only discreetly, which is like saying that the product to be sold in the first place is the disease, this actually being the companies' aim. They sell ADHD and, in so doing, ensure the future of the anti-ADHD drug they market. It's a matter of convincing the public of the reality of these new diseases, by "modernizing" them through greater possibilities of inclusion and less "psychiatric," less stigmatizing, names even if they take on the veneer of known syndromes. Simple acronyms that function as trademarks are used to facilitate inclusion, identity and transmission. The acronym "TAG," for instance, is much more upbeat and reassuring than the term "anxiety neurosis." This is called *condition branding,* which is basically a policy for marketing a disease. Whereas diseases are discovered in medicine, in the new DSM-dominated psychiatry, diseases are invented. The field of affects, of anxiety in particular, but also that of behaviors, lend themselves wonderfully to this flexibility of names, of signifiers. Vince Parry, president of a communications agency who has written on pharmaceutical marketing, noted in 2003 that no therapeutic category is more hospitable to condition branding than the field of "anxiety and mood disorders," where the disease is rarely based on measurable physical symptoms and where it is open to a conceptual dimension.[108]

We thus end up with paradox: since no biological markers of mental diseases can be found, corporations remain open on a "conceptual" level while at the same time, these diseases need to be *scientifically* established. Hence the interest in remaining in a sufficiently scientific gray zone in order to give the impression of seriousness that can convince both prescribing physicians and the public, while awaiting confirmation, in order to allow flexibility in marketing. In fact, all mental illnesses are currently in this gray zone, not just the pathologies of anxiety and mood as Vince Parry cynically says.

To promote these new diseases, the alliance with end-users is very important and in the United States, corporations have sponsored an association called CHADD, *Children and Adults with Attention*

---

[108] Quoted in Ray Moynihan and Alan Cassels, *Selling Sickness: How the World's Biggest Pharmaceutical Companies Are Turning Us All into Patients* (New York: Nation Books, 2006), 61.

Deficit Hyperactivity Disorder, which plays a very important role in informing, welcoming or advising its members, patients and parents of children or adolescents with ADHD. Yet, these user associations are not solely a transmission channel for pharmaceutical companies. While they are autonomous, there is nevertheless a convergence of interests between them. Additionally, they embody a certain conception of "health democracy." Users want to decide how they are to be cared for, and, as such, they participate in all negotiations regarding the inclusion of a particular illness in the classifications of mental illnesses. They also finance studies to improve the management of diseases. They participate in campaigns to de-stigmatize the mentally ill, with the help of publicly known donors whose children also presumably suffer from ADHD. They have become an essential part of the direction of mental health policy, which is undeniably a step forward. However, trying to achieve through medical activism what science alone can't provide entails a certain number of risks: namely, conflicts of interest with pharmaceutical companies or the potential problem of representative action within a group where sometimes the most militant or extreme voices gain the upper hand. But users' associations are also highly diverse in their orientation: some for example are strongly opposed to over-prescription while others such as *Advocacy, Mental Health Europe* or *Humapsy* – an offspring of the anti-psychiatric movement – emphasize minority rights and the second-class citizenship of the mentally ill. In France, another important association, *HyperSupers TDAH France*, has a firm stance on the indisputable existence of ADHD, yet is open to multiple and diversified approaches.

In parallel to this evolution, we note that the place of expertise in psychiatry has shifted considerably over the last few decades. Until the arrival of the DSM-III in 1980, which became a bestseller and, increasingly, the world reference work for research, epidemiology, teaching and clinical practice, the primary actor in expertise was the clinician who was sovereign in diagnostic decision-making, which was not without its drawbacks given the cacophony this generated: the same patient was considered schizophrenic on one side of the Atlantic and bipolar on the other. It was impossible to harmonize the diagnostic criteria; there was no fidelity among judges, which meant that the clinical judgments of different practitioners on the same case didn't overlap. This situation obstructed scientific exchange, research and epidemiology, and it's one of the reasons why the promoters of the DSM-III abandoned the old clinic for a descriptive behavioral psychiatry, which responds much better to operational, and thus easily usable, criteria. I've described this historical turning point in my book *Tristesse Business, Le scandale du DSM-5,*[109] as has Steeves Demazeux in *Qu'est-ce que le DSM, Genèse et transformations de la bible américaine de la psychiatrie*[110] and Michel Minard in *Le DSM roi, La psychiatrie américaine et la fabrique des diagnostics.*

Since expertise has shifted from the clinician to the manual, psychiatric diagnoses are within everyone's reach, allowing for self-diagnosis. Some of them are thus used in the dialogues of Hollywood productions. Such is the case with *The Social Network*, released in 2010, which presents itself as a fiction, though David Fincher describes in it the astonishing rise of Mark Zuckerberg and Facebook, the first, highly controversial social network. We learn that the inventor of this social network, which has enjoyed worldwide success and theoretically allows for universal virtual communication, suffered from "social phobia." We are well into the era of psychomarketing, to borrow the term Mikkel Borch-Jacobsen used in *La Fabrique des folies, De la psychanalyse au psychopharmarketing.*

For several years now, many books have been written by investigative journalists, by doctors or even by insiders who've held positions of responsibility in the pharmaceutical industry to denounce the pharmaceutical industry and its methods, and who, as "informers," have decided to expose its marketing methods and goals. John Virapen's book, *Side Effects, Death: Confessions of a Pharma-Insider,*[111] translated into French under the eye-catching title, *Médicaments, Effets secondaires: la Mort,* is particularly interesting for our purposes. It seems that this former pharmaceutical executive decided to launch a whistle-blowing campaign against his former employer when, as the father of a young child, he learned that companies would increasingly "go after" children and promote ADHD and the medications used to combat it. John Virapen's damning testimony corroborates other investigations. We discover that the nature of the pharmaceutical indus-

---

[109] Patrick Landman, *Tristesse Business, Le scandale du DSM* (Paris: Max Milo, 2013).
[110] Steeves Demazeux *Qu'est-ce que le DSM, Genèse et transformations de la bible américaine de la psychiatrie* (Paris: Ithaque, 2013.)
[111] John Virapen, *Side Effects: Death. Confessions of a Pharma-Insider* (Texas: Virtualbookworm.com Publishing, 2010).

try has changed significantly since the 1950s, 1960s and even 1970s. At that time, they provided valuable services that benefited patients, especially those with long-term mental illness. However checkered the record they left, the products manufactured by the firms had an immediate and direct application in daily practice and they contributed substantially to improving the living conditions of some patients. In addition, research on new molecules and studies were carried out in collaboration with academics and high-level researchers, driven by a concern to improve public health.

Everything changed in the 1980s, when the pharmaceutical industries became totally removed from any public service mission, to which they had been partly contributing in the past. The financialization of these industries oriented them toward the sheer quest for profit, leading to a phenomenal development of psycho-marketing and to aggressive, dubious, even illegal commercial practices, such as concealing negative studies or certain side effects. Over the past twenty years or so, a voice has been raised against these illegal or dangerous practices with convincing scientific arguments: the voice of Professor David Healy, author of numerous books including *The Antidepressant Era* and *Psychiatric Drugs Explained*.[112] His website lists information on the risks of psychotropic drugs and disseminates validated, alternative information for users.[113]

With ADHD, we are obviously at the heart of these changes and social issues. Since, as I have already written, one of the pillars on which the diagnosis of ADHD is based is methylphenidate[114] — whose best-known commercial name is Ritalin — it is important to raise the question: is ADHD a creation of Big Pharma to accrue enormous profits selling Ritalin? Once you approach these questions in this way, it's hard to escape taking a political stance, in the sense that in a political debate you have to choose sides; either the side of science and evidence-based medicine or the side of subjectivity; the side of drug efficacy or the side of denouncing Big Pharma; the side of conflicts of interest or the side of the conspirators, etc.

---

[112] David Healy, *The Antidepressant Era* (Cambridge, MA: Harvard University Press, 1997); *Psychiatric Drugs Explained*, 5th edition (London: Churchill Livingston, 2011).

[113] See: https://davidhealy.org./.

[114] There are other molecules, some of which are not amphetamines, that are marketed in certain countries. But methylphenidate is the key molecule.

Most studies to date have shown that the interest and benefits of Ritalin are short- to medium-term. Recently, we've come upon a Canadian study that has followed children medicated with psychostimulants for more than ten years.[115] The conclusions don't support an improvement in school performance in the long term. The authors speak of harmful, "emotional" side effects, including a significant decline in the enjoyment of life, as well as an increase in conflicts with parents, especially among girls. All these findings pretty well demolish the notion that the prescription of Ritalin alone can lead to long-term improvements in school performance. This development is valuable because the alleged long-term improvement has been an argument for the continuation of treatment for many years.

The side effects of Ritalin are well known: insomnia, digestive disorders, cardiovascular problems and headaches, with the most worrying being its impact on growth (a loss of over 2 lbs. and almost 1/2 inch in height per year of prescription). The cruel lack of independent and quality studies done by experts without conflicts of interest leaves the field open to assertions, testimonies or rumors whose foundations are hard to measure, even if they've been propagated in good faith. Among the negative effects, it doesn't seem that taking Ritalin leads to addictive behaviors. But it's worth mentioning another common practice in adolescence: the misuse of psychostimulants before an exam or a competition in order to perform better or as an act of defiance to prove that one can do without parental protection. This misuse of psychostimulants also affects adults.

Side effects and misuse lead to litigation. Already in 2000, there were four thousand four hundred complaints in the United States about the effects of methylphenidate, some even claiming it had caused death. The Federal Drug Administration has opened an alert procedure by making available to the public a *Medwatch Program* that allows any citizen to file a report by e-mail.[116]

Apart from the very important problem of side effects, critics are speaking out against what they call the "obedience pill," "the pill of

[115] Janet Currie, Mark Stabile, and Lauren Jones, "Do Stimulant Medications Improve Educational and Behavioral Outcomes for Children with ADHD?" *Journal of Health Economics 37* (2014), 58-69.

[116] See: https://www.fda.gov/safety/medwatch-fda-safety-information-and-adverse-event-reporting-program.

parental abdication." Karl Marx said that religion was the opium of the people, meaning that it was used to prevent the poor and the exploited from becoming aware of their condition and to fight against the exploiters in return for future consolation, the promise of Paradise. Can we use this metaphor to talk about Ritalin, perceived as deriving from social, educational, pedagogical problems and inequalities at the origin of many hyperactive behaviors? And if we find cerebral modifications in some children labeled ADHD, why not invoke the responsibility of their history, especially if it's one fraught with abandonment, violence and stress that are known to leave traces in the brain? Many emotional events that occur in the first years of life, but also break-ups, symbolic distortions permeating the language the child hears (such as lies about filiation) – all of these factors can lead to behavioral disturbances and leave traces in the brain's functioning. But this doesn't mean that an abnormality in the brain is necessarily at the origin of these behaviors. Those who think this is always the case are in fact supporters of a current called naturalism. In its extreme reductionist version, this current advocates that there's nothing else but nature.

On the other hand, there are also many testimonials of gratitude for Ritalin: with it, the child becomes unrecognizable, calm, collected, and his school performance becomes satisfactory, even excellent. In consultation we sometimes hear of such "miracles." And it can happen that the improvement continues after Ritalin is stopped, even if hyperactivity sometimes returns.

In my experience, there is no correlation between a match-up with the behavioral profile of ADHD and the success of the prescription. In other words, just because a child perfectly fits the ADHD description, it doesn't mean that he or she will automatically find relief from symptoms by taking the medication. It's also true that children without a clear ADHD profile may benefit from treatment with Ritalin. The success of the prescription likely depends on various genetic and environmental factors and the therapeutic alliance, but also on the reasons for the hyperactivity and the nature of the treatment, apart from the medication. A Ritalin prescription, when it offers sudden and unexpected relief, is often criticized for leading to a demotivation of the parents. This criticism may seem misplaced and perfectionistic, but this is not the case. In fact, many studies have shown that taking medication alone is not effective in the medium or long term, as the immediate benefits quickly fade away without psychological support for the children and their parents, accompanied by social work. Some say the effectiveness of the medication generally lasts only a few weeks.[117]

Large-scale prescribing and marketing have fostered the illusion that a problem as complex as hyperactivity can be solved by a pill. This is false and absurd, but it's also the result of the implicit theory that ADHD is a disease of brain origin, causing a chemical imbalance that the drug would aim to compensate.

So what can we conclude about ADHD medications? We are unfortunately in a context of psycho-marketing, conflicts of interest, corruption, ideological a priori, expert quarrels and studies that are hard to interpret, since most are biased or insignificant. One can't, I believe, be totally opposed to the drug treatment of hyperactivity, nor totally in favor of it. ADHD is likely to be over-diagnosed and it leads to over-prescription, as has been proved for years by experience in different countries. The request for a prescription also comes from the public, which is hearing more and more about Ritalin and ADHD. It's necessary to resist this "machine" supported by powerful interests, without falling into alarmism, and to maintain the guardrail that is the strict framework of first-line prescription, reserved for hospital patients. In severe cases of hyperactivity where intense functional repercussions put the patient's future in doubt, a prescription for medication is indicated. This recommendation should only be made, though, after less invasive measures have failed to produce any respite in the symptoms and if it is stipulated by a physical examination. In addition, a prescription must never be administered in isolation and only as a part of a therapeutic project adapted to the singularity of the case. Just as importantly, practitioners must adhere to stopping the drug regimen when the patient stabilizes, because medication is *only* a trajectory stabilizer and is in no way curative. If these guidelines are followed, then medication can represent indisputable progress. But we also need to organize a follow-up, or what used to be called guidance, in the aftermath of this segment of the treatment. This is doubly important because there is some vagueness about the long-term effects of medication on the brain. Finally, I believe that the practice

---

[117] Studies showing the benefits of comprehensive care can be found on *L'association TDA/H Belgique* website: https://www.tdah.be/tda-h/prise-en-charge/.

of psychiatry cannot escape an *idiosyncratic dimension* conceived as a way of working that suits each individual patient who will invariably display unique types of reactions and modes of behavior as well as specific bodily dispositions or unusual reactions to a particular medication or substance. In other words, psychiatry should return to a clinic of the subject.

Chapter 8: From Neuroimaging to "Neuromania"

The use of images from functional brain imaging is a striking and increasingly common phenomenon at psychiatric conferences and congresses, including the annual symposium of the American Psychiatric Association. As Dr. Mathew Crawford points out, "Neuro-talk is often accompanied by a picture of a brain scan [computerized tomographic image], that fast-acting solvent of critical faculties."[118] And it's frequently those who speak about ADHD who resort to this practice.

The properties of the image have been known to advertisers and communication professionals for a very long time. It is said that an image can speak louder than words; it sometimes has a strong force of conviction, a power of proof greater than an argument. Moreover, an image of the brain is not an image like any other. The brain retains a halo of mystery and any image that lifts the veil (even a little) on this mystery is fascinating, especially when it appears in 3D. But what are these images that some child psychiatrists or certain psychiatrists use immoderately in reality? For the most part, they are photos taken from neuroimaging examinations.

Simplifying as much as possible, we can distinguish two types of techniques to measure brain activity. We can construct images of the brain from its metabolic activity, such as the consumption of oxygen or of another substance such as glucose, in order to obtain, indirectly, a measure of the activity of neurons and of certain brain regions. Functional Magnetic Resonance Imaging (fMRI) and Proton Emission Tomography (PET) scans are, strictly speaking, the techniques we have of brain imaging and give the most "telling" and spectacular images available. These are the same images found in scholarly presentations of pharmaceutical company advertisements or in books for the broad

---

[118] Mathew B. Crawford, "The Limits of Neuro-Talk: On the Dangers of a Mindless Brain Science," *The New Atlantis*, Winter 2008, https://www.thenewatlantis.com/publications/the-limits-of-neuro-talk.

public. The second category, which includes electro-encephalography and magneto-encephalography, provides direct measurements of electrical activity in the brain. These techniques are very useful, particularly for detecting brain tumors or in epilepsy. However, they are less popular with "neuro-speakers" because they don't provide precise information on the origin and cerebral location of the neuronal activities that they collect.

The vast majority of experiments using neuroimaging in psychiatry are based on the following principles and methodology: they involve gathering information on cerebral localization (what are called cerebral substrates) and different cognitive functions such as attention, perception, memory, etc.

But before demonstrating the need to separate achievements from speculations in the field of neuroimaging applied to psychiatry, I'd like to remind you that the human brain is extremely complex and the more science advances, the more this complexity is confirmed. In the human brain there are 10 to the power of 11 nerve cells,[119] called neurons. In addition, each neuron is connected to other neurons with approximately ten thousand connections. Furthermore, each neuron is capable of receiving signals called synaptic signals from about ten thousand additional neurons, to which it may or may not respond after the signals it receives have been integrated by its cellular body. And apart from neurons, there are other cells in the brain such as glial cells, whose role has yet to be explained.[120]

There is a long-standing theory that seeks to locate cognitive functions, the so-called mental faculties, in specific areas of the brain. Invented by an anatomist, physician Franz Josef Gall (1758-1828),[121] "phrenology" (which had its hour of glory in the 19th century), was comprised of three hypotheses: 1) the human mind can be broken down into mental components distinct from each other; 2) these men-

---

[119] Or one hundred billion.

[120] Glial are non-neuronal cells located in both the peripheral and the central nervous system (the brain and spinal cord) whose structure and function are quite different than nerve cells (neurons).

[121] Franz Joseph Gall (1758-1828) was a German anatomist and physiologist who pioneered ascribing cerebral functions to various localized areas of the brain. He also invented phrenology, which hypothesized that the shape and contours of the skull affect the development of the various regions of the brain and through the skull's examination, individual mental faculties and character traits could be determined.

tal components situated at the base of the mental faculties are located in the brain in identifiable and specific areas; and 3) these specific brain regions are correlated with topographical features, themselves specific, visible on the surface of the skull. It's important to note that this last proposition gave rise to ideological formulations unacceptable today for their racism.

The phrenologists of the time tried to relate the size and shape of skulls to character or personality traits with the help of statistics. Obviously – and fortunately – all these theoretical meanderings are obsolete, but phrenology dominated psychiatry for a good part of the 19th century. Some people opposed the theory from the beginning, notably the French physician and biologist Pierre Flourens (1794-1867). According to this scholar, the brain possesses an integrating apparatus and is not just the sum of a juxtaposition of specific modules. Phrenological theories received important support, notably thanks to Broca and Wernicke's discoveries on the localization of language centers after observation and dissection of brain-damaged patients.[122] With these discoveries, the functional specificity of brain regions – the fact that certain regions of the brain are dedicated to specific functions – regained its centrality.

Since then, many other theories have flourished, but phrenology, purged of its excesses, has an offspring: *neophrenology*,[123] which seeks to locate cognitive functions – such as memory, attention and language – in cerebral areas with the help of neuroimaging. The functions are divided into increasingly numerous subsets in an attempt to delimit the purest possible cognitive functions and to locate them. This race to localize resulted in absurdities such as the claim to have found the seat of moral judgment or empathy.[124] In reality, the cogni-

---

[122] Carl Wernicke (1848–1905) was a German physician and psychiatrist known for his research into the pathological effects of brain diseases and the study of receptive aphasia, in which individuals have difficulty understanding written and spoken language. Pierre Paul Broca (1824–1880) was a French physician known for his research of a region of the frontal lobe involved in language. His work revealed that the brains of patients with aphasia contained lesions in a particular part of the cortex.

[123] Neophrenology is a pejorative but apt term to describe the theory of modularity, which proposes that the brain has specialized regions for different cognitive processes.

[124] As an example of many such articles see: Keith J.Yoder and Jean Decety, "The neuroscience of morality and social decision-making," *Psychology, Crime, and Law* 24, no. 3 (2018), 279-295.

tive entities that one seeks to localize have no scientific validity; they are either constructions related to culture and the paradigms that dominate it or they are "old entities" of psychology, faintly refreshed by more up to date names. For example, in *Le cerveau n'est pas ce que vous pensez*,[125] the authors Guillaume, Tiberghien and Baudoin ask a very pertinent question: why hasn't anyone yet proposed using brain imaging to locate the regions responsible for greed, described as a mental faculty by Gall, the inventor of phrenology? This example shows that the division of mental functions is most often dependent on theories, moral judgments or historically dated ideological and cultural positions, and that it's not a matter for science. It's accepted, for instance, that perception, memory or attention are distinct cognitive entities and that they can be studied experimentally in an independent way. In reality, there is no scientific proof that these entities are independent of each other. If we take attention as an example and divide it into subsets, we'll be able to distinguish joint attention, visio-spatial attention and sustained attention.[126] But this doesn't solve the question of the validity of this entity called attention. Moreover, a classification of cognitive functions is no substitute for scientific validation.

Consequently, when we talk about attention disorders as in ADHD, we need to be aware that we are discussing a hypothetical construction, nothing more. The difficulties here become even more complex when the inherent ambiguity of language leads to confusion. For example, "consciousness" designates at once the supposed cognitive entity and a part of this entity such as alertness. Moreover, the division of the mind into distinct modules called cognitive functions is

---

[125] Fabrice Guillaume, Guy Tiberghien and Jean-Yves Baudoin, *Le cerveau n'est pas ce que vous pensez : images et mirages du cerveau* (Presses Universitaires de Grenoble (PUG), 2013). Guillaume is a professor and research psychologist and the director of the Department of Cognitive and Experimental Psychology at Université Aix Marseille in France. Tiberghien is a cognitive psychologist and honorary professor at the Institut universitaire de France. Baudouin is a professor in the department of developmental psychology at Université Lumière Lyon-2 in France.

[126] Joint attention is the shared focus by two individuals on the same object. It is achieved when one person alerts another to an object by pointing at it or through other verbal or non-verbal indications. Visio-spatial attention is the ability to selectively process visual information through prioritizing an area within the visual field. Sustained attention is the ability to focus on an activity or stimulus over a long period of time even if there are other distractions present.

the basis for the theory called modularism,[127] which has not received definitive confirmation. Attempts, however, to locate these hypothetical modules are growing exponentially, demonstrating the considerable weakening of experimental methodological rules.

Some have drifted even further away from the rigor required for any experimental methodology. Ever since traditional clinical observation has been supplanted by the descriptive record of behaviors (under the influence of the DSM method), cerebral zones have been looked at in order to locate the origin of certain behaviors or groups of behaviors. But in fact, these attempts to locate zones within the brain that host the source of behaviors have hit an impasse. There is no unity between a behavior, a cognitive function and a brain area. It is therefore impossible to locate these cognitive functions in the brain (as anatomical modularism claims to do) and to precisely define these functions even when they are conceived of without an anatomical substrate (as in functional modularism). Therefore, anatomical modularism and functional modularism remain unvalidated theories. Furthermore, modularism is opposed by another equally hypothetical theory, that of distributed brain functioning. According to this hypothesis, cognitive functions have no precise locations in the brain, but rather, their substrate is distributed in different brain areas connected to each other. There is a distributed nature to brain activities, an overlap between areas and redundancy: in other words, the same areas are activated by the setting in motion of different cognitive functions. Accordingly, a cerebral zone does not have a strict functionality, it is not dedicated to a cognitive function, there is no memory zone or attention zone for example. There is a distribution of brain function that is made possible by the considerable number of connections between the different neurons, the well-known synapses. In this theory of the distributive functioning of brain activity, we come to doubt distinctions that have long been commonly accepted in psychology, such as the distinction between motricity and perception. Even the motor cortex would not have specific responses. But Guillaume, Tiberghien and Baudoin explain that "the neurons of the motor cortex are sensi-

---

[127] Modularism is the belief that a system such as the brain operates as a group of interconnected but separate modules which are responsible for different functions such as language.

tive to mnestic [memory related] variables"[128] and that, consequently, memory would intervene in motor skills. In other words, an fMRI image of the brain that locates a brain tumor is a valuable aid to clinical diagnosis, an indisputable benefit of scientific progress; but an fMRI image that locates the "center of empathy" is sheer illusion, a speculation that is a form of scientism.

I've mentioned *psycho-marketing*, which seeks to sell new diseases, in particular ADHD. Additionally, there's *neuro-marketing*, a commercial interest in the brain which is correlated with what Professor Raymond Tallis has called "neuromania," invoking the brain in relation to all human behavior. The British professor, who teaches at the University of Manchester, has conducted clinical neuroscience research throughout his career. In his book *Aping Mankind: Neuromania, Darwinitis and the Misrepresentation of Humanity*, he denounces scientism, exacerbated Darwinism and the distorted representation of humanity that reigns in certain neuro-scientific circles.[129] He convincingly argues that it is not the brain that thinks, but a subject that thinks. Tallis thus becomes the defender of a certain conception of the humanities and being human. He fears that neuro-marketing may dangerously change certain values when a functional MRI is used not for therapeutic reasons – to treat a person with a disease – but to try to better understand the behavior of the average consumer in order to better meet their unmet needs, or to manipulate them. In the same way, neuromania can lead us to consider that social inequalities boil down to cognitive inequalities, inequalities in brain functioning. This can go so far as to justify the following fact in the name of "brain inequality": if you're a Black child in the United States with parents from a disadvantaged social background, cramped housing, frequent parental quarrels, or parents who are separated, you are six times more likely to be diagnosed with ADHD under equal screening and treatment conditions than if you're a white child from a well-off background, with parents who live together in comfortable housing.[130]

---

[128] Op. cit., 20.

[129] Raymond Tallis, *Aping Mankind: Neuromania, Darwinitis and the Misrepresentation of Humanity* (New York: Routledge, 2014).

[130] Jude Mary Cénat, Camille Blais-Rochette, Catherine Morse et al., "Prevalence and Risk Factors Associated with Attention-Deficit/Hyperactivity Disorder Among US Black Individuals: A Systematic Review and Meta-analysis," *JAMA Psychiatry*, 78, no. 1 (2021),

Who would dare to invoke the sole responsibility of the brain in the face of such disproportion?

To illustrate the theoretical excesses of "neuromania," I'll mention two highly symptomatic examples that appear in many books. Firstly, a certain researcher named Semir Zeki, from University College London, has endeavored to explore through functional MRIs what we experience when we contemplate a work of art.[131] He has sought to locate in the brain the center of aesthetic emotion! This presumes that the impact of a work of art could be detached from the values of the subject contemplating it, its history, the cultural environment, and many other things, and could simply be reduced to the activation of a neuronal circuit. The second example has made headlines in recent years: an article in the *New York Times* on November 11, 2007, reported that neuroscientists, science analysts, policy analysts and marketing professionals came together following an experiment on a group of volunteers who had undergone an MRI.[132] Their objective was to evaluate the MRI responses prompted by the exposure to images and speeches of candidates for the 2008 U.S. presidential election. The avowed goal of these experiments was to demonstrate the cerebral determinants of our political choices! Obviously, this experiment was a fiasco but it's indicative of a certain conception of brain research, which could be described as mercantile and manipulative.

It's clear that scientists, clinicians and other ADHD advocates, with highly diverse convictions, are generally light years away from these purely profit-oriented goals of conquering the brain market. And yet they are impregnated by neuromania adhering (more or less) to the false principles opposed by Professor Tallis. For instance, if our behaviors are the product of what happens in our brains, then it means that everything that happens in our brains has its origin in our brain. This idea is patently absurd: it's obvious that what happens in our brain can have environmental, linguistic, perceptual, social, cultural

---

21-28. The calculation (six times greater) takes into account the percentage of Blacks in the US population compared with Whites and the social and economic factors predisposing to ADHD as presented in this study.

[131] Zeki is a professor of neurasthenics at University College London. As an example of his work see: *Inner Vision: An Exploration of Art and the Brain* (Oxford and New York: Oxford University Press, 1999).

[132] Marco Iacoboni et al., "This Is Your Brain On Politics," *New York Times*, Nov. 11, 2007, https://www.nytimes.com/2007/11/11/opinion/11iht-edbrain.1.8281355.html.

and other diverse origins. Reducing thought to what happens in the brain is equally absurd because of interaction and over-determination, a pluri-determinism to our thinking. How could we imagine that we could read someone's thoughts with the help of a scan of their brain? It's impossible, except in a reductionist vision. The brain is a dynamic organ, and when someone thinks, it's not that specific neural circuits are activated and could allow us to know the content of that person's thoughts thanks to the localization of these circuits. Consequently, if we put someone in a functional MRI device and measure their brain activity at the very moment we ask them to think about something, it turns out that the present thoughts aren't independent of the thoughts and experience that preceded them. The content of thought would likely be different if we ask someone to think about a house at the instance t and then again at the instance $t + 2$ hours: they won't necessarily think about the same house. *Thoughts cannot be read using functional MRIs.* This revolutionary method remains an indicator of brain and cognitive functioning thanks to a reliable marker, but it's certainly not a mind-reading device.

The mystery remains as to how the brain produces mind. But the dynamic perspective is radically opposed to a reductionist perspective. As Tiberghien writes, "The dynamic perspective obliges us to consider that the brain is cerebral in two ways, 'cerebrated' in the sense that neurocognitive states are decisive for mental life, and 'cerebrating' in the sense that it undergoes the continuous and dynamic incorporation of experiences."[133]

Another widely held misconception is to equate and confuse correlation with causality. It's this confusion that gives rise to jokes by the comedian Coluche,[134] such as: "When you're sick, you should definitely not go to the hospital: the probability of dying in a hospital bed is ten times greater than in your bed at home." As absurd and improbable as it may seem, some so-called scientific commentaries, and especially in their dissemination to the general public, blithely mingle the correlation found between two variables that evolve in parallel and a causal link. These dysfunctions of scientific information have been masterfully denounced by Professor François Gonon in an article en-

---

[133] Op cit. in footnote 103.

[134] Coluche, the stage name for Michel Gérard Joseph Colucci (1944–1986), was a famous French comedian and film actor.

titled "Biological Psychiatry: A Speculative Bubble?" published in November 2011 in the journal *Esprit*.[135] Some commentators reporting on "scientific discoveries" concerning the brain even come to consider that a correlation is equivalent to an identity; if A and B are correlated, this implies that A and B are identical. As a general rule, the identity relationship is not explicitly asserted, but is inferred from their conclusions.

These harmful confusions and illogical forms of reasoning are found at all levels of the discourses promoting ADHD, except, perhaps, at the very highest scientific ones. But some psychiatrists, child psychiatrists and documents aimed at the general public often firmly assert that hypotheses based on correlations are causal relations. I'm thinking here of the examples in which dyes in food or the exposure to certain metals are deemed to be the cause of ADHD.

In conclusion, I think that the normal cerebral and psychological development of a child lies at a crossroads where endogenous factors (the subject's singular share of genetic, cognitive and psychic characteristics) intersect with exogenous ones (their biological, linguistic, alimentary, social and relational environment). ADHD obliterates any possibility of dealing with the complexity of the so-called polyfactorial (the play of multiple factors) that overdetermines a mental pathology or a symptom such as hyperactivity by virtue of its theoretical foundations. Nevertheless, the latest scientific discoveries seem to confirm the polyfactorial hypothesis. This is notably the case in genetics, which has long been the very locus of determinism, where it is now understood that factors of genetic vulnerability are not always transformed into the expression of a disease claimed to be a "phenotype." The expression or non-expression of a gene is dependent on environmental factors in the broadest sense of the term: this is schematically the theory of epigenetics. Both vulnerability factors, said to be primary factors, and the factors preventing clinical expression, called secondary maintenance factors, are most likely a mix of somatic and psychological factors.

Through these observations, we can say that the concept of ADHD isn't merely a catch-all term likely to be over-diagnosed, nor

---

[135] François Gonon, "Biological Psychiatry: A Speculative Bubble?" *Esprit* 11 (2011), 54-73, https://www.cairn-int.info/article-E_ESPRI_1111_0054--biological-psychiatry-a-speculative.htm.

is it merely a chimera based on a description of behaviors. It is also an obstacle to the scientific understanding of hyperactivity, because it is entrapped within closed and purely physiopathological explanatory models. ADHD is a pure product of the DSM methodology and it's becoming more and more evident that this methodology leads to dead ends.

Faced with these dead ends, two paths are emerging. The first is that of giving up on the DSM in favor of even more biological, physiological criteria. This is the path chosen by the National Institute of Mental Health, the world's largest institution devoted to research in the field of mental illness. Its former director, Thomas Insel, stated in April 2013, when the DSM-5 was released, that the manual was obsolete and he trusted another, more operative reference system for research, the *Research Domain Criteria*.[136] Another path could be that of the polyfactorial approach, because the screening, evaluation and especially the choice of treatment for hyperactivity depend closely on the idea one has of it. The polyfactorial theory is much more heuristic while it is incompatible with the increasingly widespread idea of either treatment with amphetamines, or nothing. Moreover, the polyfactorial theory follows in the wake of the cautious conception of causality that prevailed before the dominance of the DSM's single-minded thinking: namely that mental illnesses stem from a causal triptych — biological, psychological and social (or the biopsychosocial model). Indeed, mental illnesses are 100 percent biological, 100 percent psychological and 100 percent social!

---

[136] Research Domain Criteria is a project of the National Institute of Mental Health (NIMH) and aims to create a new conceptual framework for understanding and treating mental disorders by applying modern research in genetics, neuroscience and behavioral science.

Chapter 9: Evidence-based Medicine

ADHD is emblematic of many of the issues facing child psychiatry and psychiatry today. After criticizing the neurodevelopmental explanatory model of ADHD – that is, the reductively conceived notion that ADHD is caused by an abnormality in brain development – I would now like to address two other questions that seem central to me. The first concerns the general conceptual framework through which the treatments, practices and recommendations of official bodies such as the National Institute for Care and Health Excellence (NICE) in Great Britain and the Haute Autorité de Santé (HAS) in France have been conducted over the last thirty years. Increasingly distrustful of practitioners, these guidelines govern how users (i.e. patients) should be treated. In France, the HAS announced its recommendations concerning ADHD for general practitioners in January 2015. This conceptual framework is named Evidence-Based Medicine (EBM) in English and, in French, either "médecine fondée sur des preuves ou des faits" or "médecine fondée sur des faits probants (MFF)" (respectively, "medicine grounded in proofs or facts" or "medicine grounded in convincing, or conclusive, facts").

How is evidence-based medicine defined? According to Sharon E. Strauss and W. Scott Richardson, "Evidence-based medicine (EBM) requires the integration of the best research evidence with our clinical expertise and our patient's unique values and circumstances."[137] A priori, it sets a goal which, if not ideal, is at the very least optimal, since it is meant to ensure that the most clinically competent practitioner uses the latest validated scientific data to care for patients, taking into account their habits, values, individual expectations and the level of evolution and severity of their pathology. This evidence-based medicine has relevance in somatic medicine, in both education and in practice,

---

[137] Sharon E. Strauss and W. Scott Richardson, *Evidence-Based Medicine*, 4th edition (New York: Elsevier, 2007).

especially since access to the latest scientific data is greatly facilitated by the internet. Indeed, some websites are dedicated to information on evidence-based medicine where it is easy to find numerous databases, collections of articles, studies or meta-analyses.[138]

How does this ideal scheme suggested by the definition of evidence-based medicine apply to psychiatry in general and ADHD in particular? This is a complex question we'll try to answer by simplifying it without betraying the issues at stake.[139]

Randomized or controlled clinical trials are the keystone here. A randomized controlled trial or randomized clinical trial is a type of scientific study used in medicine and more recently in economics. It is the gold standard for clinical trials. Randomized clinical trials are often used to test the effectiveness of several therapeutic approaches in a patient population. They can also collect information on the side effects of treatments. For example, two groups of patients with a specific pre-existing mental illness are randomly assigned. One group receives a new drug researchers want to test, the other receives a treatment already known. One then compares the results at specific times, using structured interviews and standardized tests. Side effects are also compared. It's important that patients are randomly assigned to each group because this ensures that factors that may influence treatment, such as the intensity of the disorder or sensitivity to side effects, are equally likely to be present in each group. In addition, the principle of the so-called "double blind study" is utilized: that is, neither the patients nor the experimenters know which group is receiving the new treatment and which group is receiving the already-known treatment. Both patients and experimenters are left in ignorance to avoid the biases that knowing could cause (refusals, suggestions, various reactions and so forth). Using this method, one can also compare chemical treatments and psychotherapeutic treatments or psychotherapeutic treat-

---

[138] A meta-analysis is a statistical approach combining the results of a series of independent studies on a given problem; meta-analysis allows for a more precise analysis of data by increasing the number of cases studied and drawing an overall conclusion. This approach is widely used in medicine for overall interpretation of sometimes contradictory clinical studies. It also makes it possible to detect methodological biases in the studies analyzed.

[139] All of the questions raised by the application of the principles of evidence-based medicine to the field of psychiatry have been listed in a reference book. See: Brian S. Everitt and Simon Wessely, *Clinical Trials in Psychiatry* (Hoboken: Wiley LTD, 2008).

ments using different techniques. A priori, one can view this method as scientifically based: hypotheses are advanced, tested, experimental proof established and then they can be adjusted depending on the results. Furthermore, the random distribution of standardized tests can be utilized with the aim of reducing the biases linked to the choices and attitudes of the experimenters.

Let's imagine the following: two hundred subjects labeled ADHD according to the DSM-5 criteria are randomly assigned to two groups of one hundred patients. One of the groups is followed and treated by a psychotherapeutic method alone, the other exclusively by taking psycho-stimulants. The course of the treatment is compared after three, six, twelve months and so on. Then conclusions are drawn about the relative effectiveness of these two therapeutic methods as well as their limitations and side effects. The medical rule of thumb is to always weigh the pros and cons, to strike the proverbial balance between benefits and risks of a treatment.

Many criticisms of this method and thus of the application of evidence-based medicine to psychiatry are formulated by asking whether randomized clinical trials are the gold standard or a golden calf,[140] or why most of the research findings that are published are false.[141]

The first reservation with respect to randomized clinical trials in psychiatry concerns the patients who are included as subjects in these studies. Most of the time they are hand-picked and not representative of the actual patient population. I can attest to this, having been involved in several studies. The inclusion criteria are very strict. For example, for the purposes of the study, only patients who do not present several concomitant pathologies may be selected, which means excluding most elderly patients. In 2002, a study by Mark Zimmerman showed that approximately 85 percent of patients in daily psychiatric practice are likely to be unqualified to participate in these studies.[142] While this figure may seem exaggerated, the fact remains that the sub-

---

[140] This question appears in the humorous and very evocative title of Ted J. Haptchuck's article, "The Double Blind Randomized Placebo Controlled Trial: Gold Standard or Golden Calf," *Journal of Clinical Epidemiology* 54 (2004), 541-549.

[141] John P. Ioannidis, "Why Most Published Research Findings Are False," *PLoSMedicine* 2, no. 8 (August 2005).

[142] Cited in Shannon, S. M., *Mental Health for the Whole Child: Moving Young Clients from Disease* (New York: W.W. Norton and Co., 2013), 126.

jects included in randomized clinical trials are not representative of the average patient. Thus, in studies of depression and antidepressants, patients with moderate pathologies are excluded because they are likely to respond too well to a placebo. These patients constitute a very large proportion of the standard patient population and are the primary targets for antidepressants. In addition, patients with addictions aren't generally included in antidepressant studies. This non-representativeness can be corrected but, in general, it implies a departure from the "double-blind" rule which *begins* with randomization and balance of the treatment groups to eliminate confounding and selection bias.[143]

As far as ADHD is concerned, there are many studies available, but most of them are carried out on small numbers of people and are conducted over very short periods of time. Additionally, the inclusion criteria are problematic because they exclude more disabled children, and there are many confusion-causing factors as well, especially learning disabilities and anxiety. The children labeled ADHD who participate in the studies are therefore not necessarily representative of the hyperactive patients followed in child psychiatry. In addition, it's always possible that subjects drop out of an ongoing study. As a result, they're not counted in the statistics and results. Most of the time, though, the reasons for their abandonment are not published (side effects, fatigue, mistaken inclusion, etc.). Thus, we are missing important information.

The thorny issue of conflict of interest, especially when studies are sponsored by pharmaceutical companies, is also very important. According to Jean-Claude St-Onge, who has listed several reasons to question the scientific honesty of randomized clinical trials,[144] industry-sponsored studies and research are between 3.6 and 5 times more likely to produce results favorable to the sponsor about a product competing on the market. It is known that data withholding is practiced by corporations. Studies with negative results are also not published, while those with positive results are published and then

---

[143] Selection bias arises when the observed patients are not representative of the broader patient population of interest, which may distort a measure of association in the study.

[144] Jean-Claude St-Onge, *Tous fous? L'influence de l'industrie pharmaceutique sur la psychiatrie* (Montreal: Ecosociété, 2013).

republished with only a few modifications in order to appear as new data. Among the facts of data withholding is the failure to mention the suicide rate during the trials. Public organizations and European public authorities are fighting against these aberrations. Here, two competing interests face off: that of public health, which must protect users, and that of industry, which seeks to protect patents and make very significant financial investments profitable. It is important to note other "camouflage techniques," such as the lifting of the double blind, the biased evaluation of results, the skimming of results, etc. Some say that the aberrations and arrangements are mainly related to publication, allowing the body of studies to escape these issues. This may be so, but evidence-based medicine relies on publications, and professionals have no other source of access to the information.

Another difficulty, an ethical one, concerns the so-called "control" group in psychiatry, which receives a placebo and allows comparison with the group receiving the product to be tested. But can we leave people with a pathology waiting for treatment or without treatment for the sole purpose of research? Here again, adjustments are made, but when it comes to comparing psychotherapeutic methods, Roger Perron wonders: "How can people, if there are any, who apply themselves to choose *not* to treat patients, come to believe themselves to be psychotherapists and call themselves such? How can one deliberately lie to people who are suffering and asking for help?"[145]

In addition to randomized clinical trials, evidence-based medicine places importance on guidelines. Regarding ADHD screening, some guidelines are consequently already published for use by professionals in the French National Education system. Yet, the eight-page booklet distributed by the Académie de Paris only takes into account the arguments of ADHD advocates, without the slightest reservation.[146]

---

[145] Quoted by Frédéric Advenier in *L'Évaluation des psychothérapies et de la psychanalyste* (Amsterdam: Elsevier Masson, 2011). Roger Perron is a French psychologist and psychoanalyst and author of many books and articles in both fields. For an example of his writing in English concerning research see: "How to Do Research? Reply to Otto Kernberg," *International Journal of Psychoanalysis* 87, pt. 4 (August 2006), 927-37.

[146] "Les enfants avec un Trouble Déficit de l'Attention/Hyperactivité et leur scolarité," http://www.tdahfrance.fr/IMG/pdf/plaquette_amenagements_tdah.pdf.

Nevertheless, the validity of the guidelines is increasingly debated. A study shows that most guidelines are biased by conflicts of interest.[147] But conflicts of interest aren't the only obstacle to applying evidence-based medicine in psychiatry. There are also factors specific to psychiatric practice that are just as, if not more, important.

Randomized clinical trials apply very well to drug treatments such as chemotherapies as well as to behavioral therapeutic techniques. But the application of all therapies that involve speech and transference (so-called psychoanalytical, psychodynamic or interpersonal therapies) are subject to debate and controversy. In a number of mental illnesses, in particular the pathologies of anxiety, angst and depression (in minor, moderate or medium forms), interpersonal psychotherapy should be the first-line treatment. Its effectiveness has long been known, although it isn't precisely clear how it works. In more serious pathologies, such as Bipolar Type-1 disorders or psychosis, these psychotherapies can also play a therapeutic role, as well as in all cases where approaches using speech can bring relief, without overestimating their healing power. But are these therapeutic methods measurable? Some people think so and have built up considerable databases to promote their effectiveness, thereby establishing an evidence-based psychotherapy, a term modeled on evidence-based medicine or "psychotherapy founded on factual evidence." But their point of view is disputed.[148] Assessment works when we can precisely delineate symptoms and cut them off in a controlled way from behaviors we call "disorders." But as soon as we widen the depth of field a little, and take an interest in the person, their context, their history, their personality and so on, the evaluation becomes more and more unreliable.

At this level the question of transference comes into play. As Freud defined it, the transference is essentially the repetition of the past onto the analyst's persona, which is merely the medium for patients' representations in the process of refinding fragments of their

---

[147] In August 2014, a global symposium was held in Oxford, England on the topic of guideline accountability in overdiagnosis, over prescription and overmedication. See: Moynihan, Ray et al. "Too Much Medicine: From Evidence to Action," *BMJ (Clinical research ed.)* 347 (Dec. 2013), https://doi.org/10.1136/bmj.f7141.

[148] See for example: John Marzillier, "The Myth of Evidence-Based Psychotherapy," *The Psychologist* 47, no. 7 (July 2004), 392-395.

history in the course of the treatment. According to Lacan, "the trans-ference is nothing real in the subject, if not the appearance... of the permanent modes according to which she constitutes her objects,"[149] which puts the analyst, from the perspective of the patient, in the posi-tion of "subject supposed to know." How can it be explained that some patients feel better as soon as they have made an appointment or phoned the psychoanalyst? Is it having taken the step, putting some-one in the position of the subject-supposed-to-know whom they are addressing, to get rid of one's symptom in order not to have to delve deeper into certain painful points in their history? I can't answer this question, but it's obvious that this favorable development bears the mark of the transference and that the authoritarian randomization that prevails in clinical trials goes against the transference, which results from a choice of the subject addressing this or that therapist rather than another, where unconscious determinations intervene.

One can certainly try to standardize the psychotherapeutic pro-cess, its evolution, its changing factors and its results as much as pos-sible, but the introduction of these research tools have consequences, costs and risks that bias therapeutic work.

Practitioners who refer to psychoanalysis often rely on both their clinical experience and case studies in the manner of Freud, who published various case studies which gave rise to countless commen-taries and debates that have enriched analytic transmission. The cases of Little Hans or Dora are, among others, emblematic of the Freudian method. Therefore what is transmitted isn't just the hypothesis of the existence of the unconscious, but a method, a process of heuristic in-vestigation of the clinic. To cite an example drawn from my experience as a child psychiatrist: I had a child in consultation who presented all the signs listed by the DSM-5 to lead me to a diagnosis of ADHD. In an interview with both parents present, the child was constantly fidget-ing. "You can see that you're bothering the doctor," said his mother. His parents blamed him for his poor academic performance and the risks to his social and professional future — because "it's essential to have work experience" — and the pain that his behavior in general

---

[149] Jacques Lacan, "Presentation on Transference," in *Ecrits: The First Complete Edi-tion in English*, trans. Bruce Fink (New York: W. W. Norton & Company, 2006), 183-4. The feminine pronoun is being used in this passage in reference to Freud's analysand Dora. [Translators' note]

caused them. I asked the father what his occupation was and wheth-er he had had formal education. He answered quite spontaneously that he'd succeeded perfectly well in life without having studied, add-ing that studies were useless. The child's reaction was immediate: he calmed down and concentrated on the consultation. But how can we transmit such an experience of the immediate but temporary cessation of symptoms when listening to a word of truth from the father? Is this a particular case, from which we can draw no possible, generalizable conclusion, or is it, on the contrary, emblematic? I don't know, but I *can* transmit the effect it had on me in my approach to certain cases of hyperactivity. And this has opened me up to new approaches that have been useful in other clinical situations. This event in my practice taught me something through its therapeutic and subjective impact. This is the heuristic investigation process of the clinic. Proponents of evidence-based medicine don't take into account this type of clinical case, because the level of evidence is very low in their hierarchy, and the narrative is biased in their view because it comes from the thera-pist alone; it also would require a degree of confirmation and an as-sessment of the probability of occurrence. In other words, it is nothing at all like a good randomized clinical trial or meta-analysis. Yet it would seem reasonable to me to apply the method of evidence-based med-icine when it's useful and necessary, for example to compare the ef-fectiveness of medications with the heuristic investigation method or in cases where it can be useful, that is in therapeutic situations where speech is elicited and heard.

One last point seems important to me, which is the question of comorbidities; that is, the association of several diseases or disorders in the same subject. It is of the utmost relevance to ADHD. Accord-ing to the consensus of experts, in fact, many children have not only ADHD but ADHD plus some other pathological profile. Especially at a very young age, they present signs and behaviors belonging to differ-ent profiles, such as anxiety disorder or oppositional defiant disorder, alongside ADHD (keeping within the strict framework of DSM-5 lan-guage). This makes the diagnostic process, but also studies, difficult, because it takes us far from the clinical "purity" desired by the research and inclusion criteria that generally exclude comorbidities. However, because comorbidities are so common, we are faced with concerns regarding the confounding factors that bias randomized clinical stud-ies. The frequency and remarkable importance of comorbidities marks the methodological limit of the purely behavioral cut-off point of the DSM. This shows the invalid, not to say arbitrary, directive and pharmaco-induced character of this approach. Of course, in some would-be redeeming defense of the method, it could be asserted that the different pathologies that make up comorbidity have different genetic origins, relating to distinct genetic substrates, but this has never been proved. For my part, I see in the frequency of comorbidities something quite different than a juxtaposition of several genetic substrates. This comorbidity is proof that we cannot shrug off the dimension of psychic reality with impunity, or the role of context, as well as the psychopathological axis of the diagnostic perspective. A symptom of hyperactivity is likely to lead to or represent the weakening or even the collapse of a part, if not the totality, of the child's relational system. This weakening, in turn, can be translated into severe anxiety disorders, with loss of sleep, symptoms in the depressive register, conduct disorders as well as learning disorders. In opposition to the idea of a well-defined ADHD "disease," this perspective reminds us that, faced with a symptom of hyperactivity, we are confronted not only with harmful behaviors, but we also have to be concerned with, and take care of, an entire person. In any case, nosographic subdivision has its limits, first of all that of the DSM-5, but all others as well.

We mustn't forget that children are children, they are developing and they don't have as many possibilities to express their suffering as adults. Motor expression is one of the most readily available and it has the merit of not going unnoticed for long, unlike other symptoms that may not draw the attention of those around them or may be denied by parents. In this instance, it's the children who quite often don't notice their own agitation or else deny it.

Chapter 10: ADHD in Adolescents and Adults

In recent years, more and more articles, studies and books from the scientific community have been suggesting that ADHD is not only a child's problem, but one suffered by a certain number of adolescents and adults who failed to be diagnosed with the disorder in childhood. Until now, studies on the progression of ADHD in children have shown that the symptoms of hyperactivity fade in adolescence and even more so in adulthood, making ADHD a predominantly childhood "disease."

It was also believed to affect three times as many boys as girls. It's interesting to note that there are completely different views on this gender disparity. Some are based on an unproven genetic hypothesis that girls are under-diagnosed because their behavioral symptoms are less pronounced. For others, advocates of explanations drawn from psychopathology and family psychological dynamics, this disparity is plausible in certain cases where the clinician detects excitement in the hyperactive boy because he feels an unconscious incestuous incitement or lure. Some have even dared to establish a parallel between infantile and "Don-Juan-like" instability.[150] Approaches to the significant difference in this prevalence between boys and girls are related to a certain conception of gender difference: either considering sex strictly from a genetic point of view or broadening the conception to include child sexuality and identity.

There seems to be a consensus now that undiagnosed, untreated ADHD does not heal spontaneously. It is believed to transform in adolescence and adulthood, changing somewhat in nature, yet remaining the same "disease." We can read a number of observations where the father of a teenager whose ADHD has just been "detected" spontaneously declares: "I was like that when I was his age." The author generally concludes that the father had ADHD and still has it,

---

[150] Jean Ménéchal and Roger Misès, *L'Hyperactivité infantile, Débats et enjeux* (Paris: Dunod, 2004), 73.

which isn't surprising since a genetic component is supposed. Explaining how a disease stays the same while presenting itself differently requires a theory. Michael T. Willoughby provides the following explanation:[151] in pathology, in the evolution of diseases, in particular ADHD, a distinction can be applied that is initially proposed in developmental theories, the distinction between homotypic and heterotypic continuity. According to François Barge and Marie-Christine Mouren, "Homotypic continuity is the persistence of the same symptoms throughout development; it is defined as a stability of the response modality. In the second, heterotypic continuity, the symptoms and behaviors reflecting the same syndrome can change throughout development; distinct groups of behaviors specific to each stage reflect a common underlying process. There is then coherence between the classes of responses which are expressed differently at each stage, but which remain related."[152] This is why adolescents and adults have the same "disease" as children: namely ADHD.

The extension of ADHD to teenagers and adults is presented as a "discovery" linked to the progress of modern research tools in psychiatry, i.e. criteriology (the search for inclusion criteria that are easily identifiable, and therefore operative),[153] epidemiology, neurocognitive evaluation tests, genetics and brain imaging, but also certain therapeutic methods. At the same time, it serves to confirm ancient intuitions as exemplified in literature; for instance in Molière's *L'Étourdi* or the character of Ménalque in La Bruyère's *Caractères*.[154] YouTube also has some very funny video sketches that "make a case for ADHD in adults." One typical example features a man who is supposed to

---

[151] Michael T. Willoughby and Patrick J. Curran, "Implications of Latent Trajectory Models for the Study of Developmental Psychopathology," *Development and Psychopathology* 15 (2003), 581-612. Willoughby teaches developmental and clinical psychology at University of North Carolina at Chapel Hill and is the author of many articles on ADHD.

[152] François Bange and Marie-Christine Mouren-Siméoni, *Comprendre et soigner l'hyperactivité chez l'adulte* (Paris: Dunod, 2009).

[153] Criteriology is the philosophical analysis of the various criteria upon which judgements of truth or falsehood are made. In clinical trials, inclusion criteria are characteristics that the prospective subjects must have if they are to be included in the study. Exclusion criteria are characteristics that disqualify prospects from participation in the study.

[154] "Ménalque, the distracted" is one of the characters in Jean de La Bruyère's (1645-1696) monumental work *Les Caractères ou les Mœurs de ce siècle*, published in 1696. Interestingly, La Bruyère located the cause of distraction in social phenomena and not in one's essential nature. [Translators' note]

leave his house to go to work but through his absent-mindedness, distraction, lack of planning, organizational deficits and clumsy attempts to correct his mistakes that only make the situation worse, causes a series of disasters that prevent him from leaving. These scenes, which remind us of Max Linder, Laurel and Hardy or Charlie Chaplin, are pure comedy, having nothing to do with psychiatric pathology.

As far as the adolescent is concerned, the emphasis is on making the diagnosis of ADHD which allows for preventative measures to be taken (such as medication and behavioral treatments) and gives parents a different perspective on their children's behavior. Everyone knows that adolescence is most often a time in life when conflicts erupt for many subjects, especially relating to school performance. Therefore the diagnosis of ADHD, that is, the existence of a mental disorder in the adolescent, is proffered as a comfort for parents. They feel that they can finally put a name to problems with concentration, risky behaviors and academic complacency. But there is a worrisome flip side to this coin: firstly, the teenager finds himself the bearer of a mental disorder which, in many cases, will result in a prescription for medication. Secondly, it would be truly naïve to imagine that the care that will be provided to combat ADHD will solve all the complex problems related to this period. In some cases, the benefits of the medication may even mask conflicts that aren't addressed, and if they're not otherwise resolved may reappear at a later date. But the most worrying consequence is the danger of stigmatization. Admittedly, a teenager in difficulty or failing at school, who engages in risky behaviors that fuel conflict with his parents, doesn't necessarily have good self-esteem. But are adolescents who are having difficulties going to gain anything by getting a psychiatric diagnosis that exonerates the parents from any responsibility, makes them alone "carry the can" for the situation, "explains" all their difficulties in childhood or almost all of them and leads them to take medication because they are considered "sick"? Not all adolescents react in the same way, but the risks of stigmatization shouldn't be underestimated.

The DSM-5 has also opened the door for pre-teens to be more easily included in the ADHD diagnosis. Remember that the DSM-5 took as a criterion for ADHD that signs of the disorder could appear before the age of twelve, whereas the DSM-IV spoke of signs appearing before the age of seven, clearly a technique for lowering the thresholds for inclusion. The diagnosis of ADHD in children is based on one condition: behavioral disorders must be identified in two different settings, usually both at home and at school, and this is determined by a questionnaire issued to parents and teachers. This condition is difficult to transpose to the adolescent's situation in middle school or high school because during this period students are faced with many teachers who generally spend relatively little time in contact with them. As a consequence, we will have to look for a history of symptoms in childhood, since we consider that the teenager with ADHD has been an undiagnosed ADHD child. But here, let's beware of suggestion and especially of any retrospective illusion that what we see in the present is perceived as having always existed. And the assessment scales are also changing, since we can't appeal to teachers, given the above-mentioned lack of contact. So we go from Conners's scales to Brown's scales.[155] The items aren't quite the same, but they are based on the same principle: the subjective survey of behavioral symptoms such as attention problems, refusal to buckle down to school tasks, distraction, the need to hurry and do several tasks at the same time, the tendency to channel surf ("zapping"), to botch everything up, impatience, etc. One is struck by the lack of specificity of these behavioral symptoms and especially by the scant differences with variations from the norm.

With such a commonly widespread pattern of behavior, ADHD is likely to be over-diagnosed, creating a large number of false positives, for which psychostimulants will be prescribed. This impression of wanting to medicalize and pathologize the behaviors of adolescence is further reinforced when one reads the signs in the "appendices" that help in the diagnosis of adolescents: "doesn't obey," "does whatever pops into his head," "doesn't listen," "can't get organized," "has multiple risky behaviors and accidents," etc. This reveals a strictly psychiatric handling of adolescence. Nowhere is it taken into account that adolescence is a period of life where the entry into sexual life is an added burden causing anxiety and frustration. Defiant attitudes are assumed to prove that one can do without parental protection, the desire arises to be "the owner of one's body," along with an ambivalent desire for independence from parents, a refusal of adult authority, and so on.

---

[155] For Conners, see footnote 79. The Brown Executive Function/Attention Scale is a set of rating tests designed to evaluate executive functions related to ADHD for children 3 to 12 years old. They can be used as a preliminary screening tool or for a more comprehensive evaluation and to monitor progress and treatment effectiveness.

This extension of the ADHD diagnosis is, in my opinion, highly abusive and unjustified. It leads to the prescription of psychostimulants without any precise criteria of duration, and carries a specific risk: some adolescents, as previously mentioned, use the medication to push their intellectual performance level during an exam or a competition. This misuse through forged prescriptions or prescription trafficking has become a problem in the United States. In France, the risk is less pronounced, thanks to the supervision of prescriptions and the awareness of this issue among health professionals, including specialists in ADHD in teenagers. Still, even in France, it can't be ruled out altogether and may become a public health problem there as well. Thus, in *L'Adolescent hyperactif*[156] Marie-France Le Heuzey correctly mentions this iatrogenic risk.

In adults, a distinction must be made between those who have been diagnosed with ADHD and treated from childhood and those who have not been diagnosed in childhood or adolescence and in whom the "disease" has taken its progressive course. It is this second group – those exhibiting a late onset of symptomatic behaviors – that are classified as adults with ADHD.

The assertion of the existence of adult ADHD has not been met with an easy consensus. Studies have been conducted on cohorts of children diagnosed with ADHD and followed over decades.[157] Some claim that, in the vast majority of cases, the symptoms of ADHD disappear spontaneously in adulthood. However, this claim has been challenged because these studies exclude children with conduct disorders or antisocial behaviors that often accompany severe forms of ADHD. Once again, we find that the reasoning is partial and biased, since it doesn't take into account the social conditions of these children, the lack of response to these adverse conditions, or the sometimes exclusively repressive responses to their antisocial behaviors, as well as the negative synergy these conditions and responses are likely to create. Is it ADHD that persists, or the disadvantaged social conditions?

---

[156] Marie-France Le Heuzey, *L'Adolescent hyperactif* (Paris: Odile Jacob, 2009). Heuzey is a psychiatrist in the child and adolescent psychopathology department at the Robert-Debré Hospital in Paris.

[157] See for example: Salvatore Mannuzza and Rachel G. Klein, "Long-term Prognosis in Attention-Deficit/Hyperactivity Disorder," *Child and Adolescent Psychiatric Clinics of North America* 9, no. 3 (July 2000), 711-726.

The distribution of ADHD in adulthood is nearly equal between the sexes, with women being exposed to the diagnosis almost at the same rate as men, unlike in childhood where the disparity between boys and girls still remains despite the fact that no convincing explanation for this difference has ever been put forward.

Diagnosis for adults according to the DSM-5 is based on the same criteria as for children and adolescents, with one difference: whereas for children, six behavioral symptoms were required – in the inattention series, in the hyperactivity/impulsivity series, or both – the DSM-5 now requires only five for adults.

The International Classification of Diseases (ICD 10) established by the World Health Organization, which is the legal reference in France, is based on different criteria, valid for both children and adolescents. First of all, the name is different: it refers to "disturbances of activity and attention." In addition, there are six criteria of inattention, in which at least three of hyperactivity and at least one of impulsivity are required. There are no subtypes, as there are in the DSM-5.[158]

The particularity of adult ADHD is based on attention disorders and instability, which can oftentimes take the form of professional or family instability. Difficulty staying in a job for a long period of time is a common problem. Assuming the role of parenthood is another which is due – in part – to the adult's projections onto and identification with the child in which they recognize themselves. Even more so than for the adolescent, we are faced with a behavioral description that is not very specific and, above all, quite extensive and indistinct in variations from the norm. Really, what adult doesn't experience attention deficits?

The issue of comorbidities is another thorny one in ADHD in adults. As I've mentioned, I do not agree with this term because it compartmentalizes symptoms into distinct and often artificial pathological units, which brings about diagnostic confusion or aggravation. It often leads to a staggering addition of anxiolytic medication for anxiety disorders, antidepressants for thymic disorders, hypnotics for sleep disorders, psychostimulants for attention disorders, etc. This leads to over-prescription with no scientific validity, while multiplying

---

[158] In the DSM-5, the term ADHD was retained with the introduction of three specific subtypes (predominantly inattentive, predominantly hyperactive-impulsive and combined), defined by the presence of excessive symptoms of inattention and/or hyperactivity/impulsivity.

the risk of side effects. The psychiatrist is no longer in contact with a person but faced, through a kind of chop-up procedure, with a tabulation of pathologies.

Studies tell us that comorbidities are extremely frequent. They affect one out of every two people diagnosed with ADHD. ADHD proponents imagine that the comorbid disorder and ADHD have a common etiology, or that ADHD represents an early manifestation of the comorbid disorder, or that ADHD and the comorbid disorder are associated in their development. These hypotheses tend to establish the validity of ADHD, instead of considering it as a symptomatic manifestation that is found in a large number of pathological situations and especially mental suffering, as witnessed by the incredible frequency of the aforementioned comorbidities.

Personality disorders are at the forefront of comorbidities, first and foremost those of so-called borderline personalities, which are characterized by major impulsivity and marked instability in emotions as well as in interpersonal relationships and self-image. This confirms the structural hypotheses of some psychoanalysts who have identified through clinical interviews and personality tests that hyperactive children quite frequently fall into the borderline state, that is to say, a psychic structure that is neither psychosis nor neurosis and which shows a lack or difficulty in structuring.

Antisocial personality is also often cited among those concerned with comorbid disorders, and hyperactive behaviors are overrepresented in this category, especially in prisons, which tends to confirm — except to the blind eyes of those who hold to the exclusive biological etiology of ADHD — that the social dimension and setting must not be forgotten in the factors favoring, predisposing and even causing ADHD.

Another comorbidity is represented by the use of alcohol, cannabis or other substances. Studies conducted in particular in the United States have shown that adults labeled as hyperactive are significantly more exposed than the normal population to the risk of substance abuse or dependence on psychoactive substances. When an adult with ADHD also exhibits so-called antisocial behaviors, the risk of abuse and dependence is even greater. How can we not see this comorbidity of ADHD and substance abuse as a new role assigned to the prescription of ADHD medications? It seems obvious that in some cases where this comorbidity is identified, the prescription of methylphenidate, which is a psychostimulant that has an amphetamine-like effect,[159] may serve the role of a product substitute, such as methadone, which is used as a replacement treatment for opioid use. If this is the case, two serious problems arise. First, substitution treatment is often a lifelong treatment, and in this case methylphenidate is no longer a simple drug use trajectory stabilizer, nor of course a curative treatment, but a new kind of replacement treatment, which marks a change in perspective. And the studies cited demonstrating the effectiveness of this kind of treatment aren't totally conclusive, while the side effects such as tics, sleep disorders or mood disorders aren't insignificant. Secondly, there is insufficient hindsight to assess the undesirable effects, but it would be interesting in the future to study the hypothesis of substitution treatment.

When I talked about childhood hyperactivity, I referred to the theories that equate hyperactivity with manic defense. Does a hyperactive adult look like an adult in a manic or hypomanic phase? If we stick to the description of behaviors, we find similarities such as agitation, the search for novelty, sensations and intensity. But in ADHD behaviors, the subject isn't in a state of omnipotence or denial, and mood swings aren't as marked. In fact, reading the description of ADHD in adults, one has the feeling of a big catch-all category that aims to occupy a large niche of behaviors at the limit of the normal, behaviors associated with pathological ones called comorbid, as well as original personalities that are a bit marginal, inventive or crying out for exclusion. Faced with such a motley mix, how can we not wonder if the ADHD adult isn't simply the prototype of the normal postmodern adult, even more than the new "bipolar" one? The latter "succeeds" when he or she is in the manic phase, but seriously fails in the melancholic phase, while ADHD adults are constantly on the lookout for the new. The latter can succeed socially only if they have mechanisms to compensate for a lack of concentration or can transform impulsiveness into an initiative so prized in certain professional circles that his or her creativity and originality can become assets.

If my hunch is right and some of the hyperactive adults embody in their own way a figure of postmodern humanity, it follows that we

---

[159] The U.S. Drug Enforcement Agency (DEA) classifies amphetamine products (which includes methamphetamine and methylphenidate) as Schedule II controlled stimulants which have a high potential for abuse and may lead to severe psychological or physical dependence.

will have more and more hyperactive adults by contagion and by conformism (thus a new social norm to which we all must submit) who present a sprinkling of behaviors and qualities as in a recipe: a dash of originality, another of flaws, a bit of creativity, some impulsiveness, a slight sense of initiative... The norm of social behavior thus created will inevitably lead to a new statistical standard. And yet the action of psycho-marketing "sells" us this "normal man" as a "disease." Perhaps the adult with ADHD will succeed where the bipolar adult, who shares many of the same symptoms but not the social acceptance, fails. And we can bet that, armed with a new sense of entitlement, the ADHD adult will steal the spotlight from the bipolar, too.

Finally, I want to emphasize the misuse of ADHD medications. This will become an increasing problem for young adults under the pressure of higher education. They're the population most at risk for the misuse of anti-ADHD substances that increase the ability to concentrate during repetitive and boring or tedious tasks. It's been shown that as academic requirements increase, so does the risk of misuse of anti-ADHD substances. Their diverted use to obtain an excitement-type pleasure, the amphetamine effect, is much rarer. It occurs only in a very small proportion of all diverted uses, because it requires a very large dose and a non-oral route of ingestion. Legal psychostimulants don't represent financial stakes comparable to drugs such as cocaine; they aren't trafficked in an organized fashion: students get them from their peers or by faking ADHD-like symptoms for a gullible or obliging doctor. Yet they are, at the end of the day, a side effect of psychomarketing, pharmaco-induced psychiatry, over-diagnosis and over-prescribing, which suggests that the difference between drugs and medication can sometimes be a very fine line in the psychiatric field. We must remember that not one psychotropic drug has ever been curative in the sense that antibiotics, or the many other drugs which exist in the pharmacopeia of physicians, have been.

The question is especially acute with regard to psychostimulants – of which methylphenidate is included – because they were first used in very different circumstances such as wars, where the aim was to obtain artificially a certain affective or emotional state and above all an effect on sleep and alertness.[160]

---

[160] Eric Bower and James Phelan, "Use of Amphetamines in the Military Environment," *The Lancet: Extreme Medicine* 362 (December 2003).

Chapter 11: Conclusion

I started this book by asking: Does ADHD exist? And at the end of my work, I can safely say: *No, ADHD does not exist.* But if ADHD does not exist, hyperactive people do exist, as do people suffering from impulsiveness and severe concentration problems. But there is no point in putting them into the catch-all category of ADHD. We must take care of them and try with them to come up with the best treatment modalities, taking into account clinical experience in listening, as well as advances in neuroscience, in particular those in neuropsychology and its possible applications in various rehabilitation techniques.

ADHD is an invention of American psychiatry and more precisely of the DSM which, taking up the old category of hyperactivity, has manufactured a chimera adapted to the prescription of psychostimulants through justifications drawn from neurocognitive psychology but arrived at without any validation.

ADHD has no scientific justification and the biological markers for ADHD as such will never be found. The rate of promotion of ADHD worldwide and its extension to new population categories brings little to improving the mental health of people with severe hyperactivity and/or severe concentration disorders. It does, however, put more and more people at risk of becoming false positives and of being unduly prescribed psychostimulants with partly unknown long-term effects, especially on a fully developing child's brain.

The promotion of ADHD, especially among teenagers and adults, is partly linked to the aims of psycho-marketing, disguised as aims of prevention and public health by deluded experts locked in their intellectual conflicts of interest or by others who become willing accomplices.

ADHD has no merit as a diagnosis. The behavioral symptoms that it lists are neither specific nor pathognomonic, and distinguishing them as variations from the norm isn't possible. Furthermore, the reliability of ADHD is very relative, since it rests on subjective assessments of behaviors that depend on the cultural, social and family context and on different tolerance thresholds. Its usefulness in improving the mental health of hyperactive people can be summed up overall in the indisputable – but questionable long-term – effectiveness of psycho-stimulants on human behavior and concentration.

ADHD has always been based on an unproven purely organi-cist theory, without regard for psychological and social factors. It is the pure product of a drift toward the "wholly biological" which has stamped a dominant one-track way of thinking on psychiatry for several decades.

ADHD is based on a conception of the disruptive child, singly responsible for certain family dysfunctions, whose disorders must be corrected and who are at risk of being stigmatized by a psychiatric diagnosis.

ADHD is a fake disease and psychostimulant medication is not the treatment for this fake disease. To believe that ADHD is a disease treated with methylphenidate is to mimic a medical reasoning that in no way applies to this ADHD-methylphenidate coupling.

ADHD is on an inexorable mission to be over-diagnosed be-cause it creates a growing social demand focused on the behaviors of children and teenagers that hamper families and educational institutions reframed as "symptoms." In this way, families and schools don't have to question themselves, thanks to the psychiatricization of the child or teenager. It contributes to psychiatricizing social, pedagogical and educational problems. It also offers a reassuring visibility, a medical pseudo-identity and a "readymade" treatment for these behaviors, which has led to its widespread backing among some users.

The diagnosis of ADHD skews epidemiological data by creating false epidemics.

ADHD is one of the crown jewels in the neuro-developmental model which, when interpreted reductively without scientific justification, shifts problems that should be the responsibility of child psychiatry toward pseudo-neurology and disability.

ADHD causes professionals to lose interest in all other models and in diversified treatment modalities that take into account the subjectivity and effects of language and speech, as well as social interventions.

While the prescription of a psychostimulant is sometimes necessary, the promotion of ADHD to the general public gives credence to the notion that all the complex problems of hyperactivity can be solved with one pill, which is an illusion and a regression in thought.

ADHD is already part of the medical culture worldwide. In the United States the National Institute of Mental Health (NIMH) refers to ADHD as a well-known developmental disorder that "begins in childhood and continues into adulthood." And although they acknowledge that the origin of the disorder is unknown, they claim that "many studies suggest that genes play a large role" while also recognizing the ongoing research into social and environmental factors. In France, the diagnosis of ADHD has all but received its authentication from the French National Authority for Health (HAS)[161] despite unquestionable efforts to break out of this paradigm. I suspect that even HAS won't be able to resist the combined pressure of certain users and of biased experts who claim to represent the consensus.

Science will sooner or later find the subtle biological mechanisms that are correlated with hyperactivity, inattention and impulsiveness. But these modules will be called something else, and will designate realities other than the one determined by these words, albeit with some overlaps. And ADHD, like so many other social constructions, will become obsolete. In fact, it has already been partly replaced by a new disease, considered as cognitive-lethargic functioning and given the name Sluggish Cognitive Tempo (SCT).[162] Correspondingly, ADHD will someday seem mostly to have embodied a fashion, a fad, one of so many in the history of psychiatry. It's in the nature of fashion, after all, to pass away...

What won't pass away is the complexity of the mental functioning of human beings and their pathologies, anchored at one and the same time in brain biology, story-telling, language and social integration. And this is what makes me optimistic.

---

[161] The Haute Autorité de Santé (HAS), or French National Authority for Health, was set up by the French government in August 2004 in order to bring together a number of activities designed to improve the quality of patient care and to guarantee equity within the healthcare system.

[162] Sluggish Cognitive Tempo (SCT) is considered an attention disorder associated with symptoms that resemble signs of inattentive ADHD: excessive day dreaming, behaving lethargically, poor memory retrieval, trouble staying alert in boring situations, slow processing of information and acting withdrawn.

Bibliography

Abramson, John. *Overdo$ed America: The Broken Promise of American Medicine*. New York: HarperCollins, 2004.

Académie de Paris. "Les enfants avec un Trouble Déficit de l'Attention/Hyperactivité et leur scolarité." Available on: http://www.tdahfrance.fr/IMG/pdf/plaquette_amenagements_tdah.pdf.

Allen, Scott. "Backlash on Bipolar Diagnoses in Children: MGH Psychiatrist's Work Stirs Debate." *Boston Globe*, June 17, 2007.

American Psychiatric Association. *Diagnostic and Statistical Manual of Mental Disorders*. Washington DC: American Psychiatric Association Publishing.

--- Diagnostic and Statistical Manual of Mental Disorders (DSM-I), 1952.

--- Diagnostic and Statistical Manual of Mental Disorders (DSM-II), 1968.

--- Diagnostic and Statistical Manual of Mental Disorders (DSM-III), 1980.

--- Diagnostic and Statistical Manual of Mental Disorders (DSM-III-R), 1987.

--- Diagnostic and Statistical Manual of Mental Disorders (DSM-IV), 1994.

--- Diagnostic and Statistical Manual of Mental Disorders (DSM 5), 2015.

Anderson, Jenny. "Decades of Failing to Recognize ADHD in Girls Has Created a 'Lost Generation' of Women." *Quartz*, January 19, 2016. Available on: http://qz.com/592364/decades-of-failing-to-recognize-adhd-in-girls-has-created-a-lost-generation-of-women/.

Anderson, Vicki and Tim Godber. *Rethinking ADHD: Integrated Approaches to Helping Children at Home and at School.* Sydney: Allen & Unwin, 2003.

Armstrong, Walter. "Will Success Rock Shire Pharma?" *Pharmaceutical Executive,* Mar. 10, 2010: 6–10.

Bakan, Joël. *Childhood Under Siege: How Big Business Targets Your Children.* New York: Free Press, 2012.

Bange, François and Marie-Christine Mouren-Siméoni. *Comprendre et soigner l'hyperactivité chez l'adulte.* Paris: Dunod, 2009.

Barkley, Russell A. "Dedicated to Education and Research on ADHD." Available on: https://www.russellbarkley.org/

--- "International Consensus Statement on ADHD, January 2002." *Clinical Child and Family Psychology Review* 5 no. 2 (June 2002): 89-111.

--- *Attention-Deficit Hyperactivity Disorder: A Handbook for Diagnosis and Treatment.* 4th edition. New York: Guilford Press, 2015.

Barkley, Russell A., et al. *ADHD in Adults: What the Science Says.* New York: Guilford Press, 2010.

Barkley, Russell A., Mariellen Fischer, Lori Smallish, and Kenneth Fletcher. "Does the Treatment of Attention-Deficit/Hyperactivity DIsorder with Stimulants Contribute to Drug Use/Abuse? A 13-Year Prospective Study." *Pediatrics* 111, no. 1 (2003): 97–109.

Behavioral Briefs: "ADHD Has Repercussions Throughout Adulthood." *Medscape,* Aug 1, 2004. Available on: http://www.medscape.com/viewarticle/488329.

Berger, Maurice. *L'Enfant instable.* Paris: Dunod, 2005.

Bergès-Bounes, Marika and Jean-Marie Forget, et al. *L'Enfant insupportable: Instabilité motrice, hyperkinésie et trouble du comportement.* Toulouse: Érès, 2010.

Bergès, Jean. *Le Corps dans la neurologie et dans la psychanalyse.* Toulouse: Érès, 2001.

Biederman, J., MC Monuteaux, E. Mick et al. "Young Adult Outcome of Attention Deficit Hyperactivity Disorder: A Controlled 10-Year Follow-Up Study." *Psychological Medicine* 36, no. 2 (2006): 167–79.

Blatchford, Peter, Anthony Russell et al. "The Effect of Class Size on the Teaching of Pupils Aged 7- 11 Years." *School Effectiveness and School Improvement* 18, no. 2 (2007): 147–172.

Blatchford, Peter, Kam Wing Chan et al., eds. *Class Size: Eastern and Western Perspectives*. London-New York: Routledge, 2016.

Borch-Jacobsen, Mikkel. *La Fabrique des folies, De la psychanalyse au psychopharmarketing*. Auxerre, France: Sciences Humaines, 2014.

Boulanger, Charles. *Contribution à l' étude de l'instabilit é mentale: Thèse pour le Doctorat en Médecine*. Paris: Imprimerie de la Faculté de Médecine, 1892.

Bourin, Michel. "History of Depression Through the Ages." *Archives of Depression and Anxiety* (May 6, 2020). Available on: https://www.peertechzpublications.com/articles/ADA-6-145.php.

Bower, Eric and James Phelan. "Use of Amphetamines in the Military Environment." *The Lancet: Extreme Medicine* 362 (December 2003): 18-19.

Brassett Harknett, Angela. "Attention-Deficit/Hyperactivity Disorder: An Overview of the Etiology and a Review of the Literature Relating to the Correlates and Life Course Outcomes for Men and Women." *Clinical Psychology Review* 27, no. 4 (March 2007): 188-210.

Carey, Benedict. "Scientists Link Gene Mutation to Autism Risk." *The New York Times*, April 4, 2012.

Cénat, Jude Mary, Camille Blais-Rochette, Catherine Morse et al. "Prevalence and Risk Factors Associated with Attention-Deficit/Hyperactivity Disorder Among US Black Individuals: A Systematic Review and Meta-analysis." *JAMA Psychiatry* 78, no. 1 (2002): 21-28.

Chen, Jianping. "Dopaminergic Mechanisms and Brain Reward." *Seminars in Neuroscience* 5, no. 5 (October 1993): 315-320. Available on: https://www.sciencedirect.com/science/article/abs/pii/S1044576505800387.

Clément, Celine. *Le TDA/H chez l'enfant et l'adolescent.* Bruxelles, Belgium: De Boeck, 2013.

Conners, CK, and L Eisenberg. "The Effects of Methylphenidate on Symptomatology and Learning in Disturbed Children." *American Journal of Psychiatry* 120, no. 5 (1963): 458–64.

Conners, Keith C. and Karen C. Wells. *Hyperkinetic Children: A Neuropsychosocial Approach.* Beverly Hills, CA: Sage Publications, 1986.

Conners, Keith C. *The Conners Rating Scale.* 3rd edition. New York: Pearson North America, 2008.

Conrad, Peter. "Genetic Optimism: Framing Genes and Mental Illness in the News." *Culture, Medicine and Psychiatry* 25, no. 2 (2001): 225-47.

Cortés, Javier Fenolla, Ignasi Navarro Soria, Carlota González, and Julia Sevilla. "Cognitive profile for children with ADHD by using WISC-IV: subtypes differences?" *Revista de Psicodidáctica* 20 (2015): 157-176.

Crawford, Mathew B. "The Limits of Neuro-Talk: On the Dangers of a Mindless Brain Science." *The New Atlantis*, Winter 2008. Available on: https://www.thenewatlantis.com/publications/the-limits-of-neuro-talk.

Currie, Janet, Mark Stabile, and Lauren Jones. "Do Stimulant Medications Improve Educational and Behavioral Outcomes for Children With ADHD?" *Journal of Health Economics 37* (2014): 58-69.

Da Silva, Erica et al. "Pharmaceutical Attention to the Risks of Inappropriate Use of Marijuana in the Treatment of Depression." *Research, Society and Development* 11, no. 17 (2022). Available on: https://rsdjournal.org/index.php/rsd/article/view/38877.

Demazeux, Steeves. *Qu'est-ce que le DSM, Genèse et transformations de la bible américaine de la psychiatrie.* Paris: Ithaque, 2013.

Diatkine, René, Serge Lebovici, and Michel Soulé. *Traité de psychiatrie de l'enfant et de l'adolescent.* Paris: Presses Universitaires de France, 1997.

Diener, Yann. *On agite un enfant: L'État, les psychothérapeutes et les psychotropes.* Paris: La Fabrique, 2011.

"Disability." American Psychological Association (APA). Last modified July 2022. Available on: https://apastyle.apa.org/style-grammar-guidelines/bias-free-language/disability#:.

"Drug Scheduling." U.S. Drug Enforcement Agency (DEA). Available on: https://www.dea.gov/drug-information/drug-scheduling.

Ehrenberg, Alain. "Épistémologie, sociologie, santé publique: Tentative de clarification." *Mouvements* 49, no. 1 (2007): 89-97.

Eric Suni, Eric and Alex Dimitriu. "Teens and Sleep." Washington D.C.: Sleep Foundation. Last modified March 1, 2023. Available on: https://sleepfoundation.org/sleep-topics/teens-and-sleep.

Everitt, Brian S. and Simon Wessely. *Clinical Trials in Psychiatry*. Hoboken: Wiley LTD, 2008.

Faraone, Stephen V., Michel Lecendreux, and Eric Konofal. "Growth Dysregulation and ADHD: An Epidemiologic Study of Children in France." *Journal of Attention Disorders* 16, no.7 (October 2012): 572-8. Available on: https://www.researchgate.net/publication/51547728.

"FDA Announces Shortage of Adderall." US Food and Drug Administration (FDA). 2022. Available on: https://www.fda.gov/drugs/drug-safety-and-availability/fda-announces-shortage-adderall.

Fink, Paul J. "The Challenge of Treating ADHD." *News*, April 1, 2004.

Fischman, Georges, Frédéric Advenier, et al. *L'Évaluation des psychothérapies et de la psychanalyste*. Amsterdam: Elsevier Masson, 2011.

Foucault, Michel. *Madness and Civilization: A History of Insanity in the Age of Reason*. Translated by Richard Howard. New York: Vintage-Random House, 1988.

Frances, Allen. "A Disease Called Childhood." *New York Post*, March 31, 2013. Available on: https://nypost.com/2013/03/31/a-disease-called-childhood/.

--- *Saving Normal: An Insider's Revolt Against Out-of-Control Psychiatric Diagnosis, DSM-5, Big Pharma, and the Medicalization of Ordinary Life*. New York: HarperCollins, 2013.

Freud, Sigmund. *The Interpretation of Dreams (1900-01). The Standard Edition of the Complete Psychological Works of Sigmund Freud IV–V*, edited by James Strachey. London: Hogarth Press, 1953.

Fulton, Brent D., Richard M. Scheffler, Stephen P. Hinshaw, et al. "National Variation of ADHD Diagnostic Prevalence and Medication Use: Health Care Providers and Education Policies." *Psychiatric Services* 60, no. 8 (2009): 1075–83.

Gaastra, Geraldina, Yvonne Groen et al. "The Effects of Classroom Interventions on Off-Task and Disruptive Classroom Behavior in Children with Symptoms of Attention-Deficit/Hyperactivity Disorder: A Meta- Analytic Review." *PLOS ONE* 11, no. 2 (2016). Available on: https://doi.org/10.1371/journal.pone.0148841.

Gauvrit, Nicolas. *Les Surdoués ordinaires*. Paris: PUF, 2014.

Gesell, Arnold and Frances L. Ilg. *Child Development: An Introduction to the Study of Human Growth*. New York: Harper, 1949.

Giami, Alain, Jean-Louis Korpes, and Chantal Lavigne. "Representations, Metaphors and Meanings of the Term 'Handicap' in France." *Scandinavian Journal of Disability Research*. 9, no. 34 (2007): 199-213.

Gibello, Bernard. *L'enfant agité*. Unpublished manuscript.

--- *Les Troubles de la pensée chez l'enfant instable: Dysharmonies cognitives, dyschronie et anomalies de la construction de l'espace de santé*. Victoria, AU: Papyrus, 2008.

Gilloots, Marie. *L'Hyperactivité infantile, Débats et enjeux*. Paris: Dunod, 2004.

Gonon, François. "Biological Psychiatry: A Speculative Bubble?" *Esprit* 11 (2011): pp. 54-73. Available on: https://www.cairn-int.info/article-E_ESPRI_1111_0054--biological-psychiatry-a-speculative.htm.

Guillaume, Fabrice, Guy Tiberghien, and Jean-Yves Baudoin. *Le cerveau n'est pas ce que vous pensez: images et mirages du cerveau*. Fontaine, France: Presses Universitaires de Grenoble, 2011.

Hallowell, Edward. "The Hallowell ADHD Centers." Available on: https://drhallowell.com/.

Hallowell. Edward M. and John J. Ratey. "The Story of Fidgety Philip." In *Driven to Distraction: Recognizing and Coping with Attention Deficit Disorder.* New York: Touchstone, 1994.

Haptchuck, Ted J. "The Double Blind Randomized Placebo Controlled Trial: Gold Standard or Golden Calf." *Journal of Clinical Epidemiology,* 54 (2004).

Harris, Gardiner. "Drug Maker Told Studies Would Aid It, Papers Say." *The New York Times*, Mar. 19, 2009. Available on: https://www.nytimes.com/2009/03/20/us/20psych.html.

Harris, Gardiner. "F.D.A. Finds Short Supply of Attention Deficit Drugs." *The New York Times*, Dec. 31, 2011. Available on: https://www.nytimes.com/2012/01/01/health/policy/fda-is-finding-attention-drugs-in-short-supply.html.

Healy, David. *Psychiatric Drugs Explained,* 5th edition. London: Churchill Livingston, 2011.

--- *The Antidepressant Era.* Cambridge, MA: Harvard University Press, 1997.

Healy, Melissa. "Geneticists Uncover a Key Clue to Schizophrenia." *Los Angeles Times*, Jan. 27, 2016.

Henderson, Kelly. "Teaching Children with Attention Deficit Hyperactivity Disorder: Instructional Strategies and Practices" U.S. Department of Education. 2006. Available on: https://files.eric.ed.gov/fulltext/ED495483.pdf.

Hinshaw, Stephen P. and Richard M. Scheffler. *The ADHD Explosion: Myths, Medication, Money and Today's Push for Performance*. New York: Oxford University Press, 2014.

Hoffman, Heinrich. *Struwwelpeter: Merry Stories and Funny Pictures by Heinrich Hoffman.* Project Gutenberg. Available on: https://www.gutenberg.org/ebooks/12116.

Horwitz, Allan V. *DSM: A History of Psychiatry's Bible.* Baltimore: Johns Hopkins University Press, 2021.

Iacoboni, Marco et al. "This Is Your Brain On Politics." *The New York Times*, Nov. 11, 2007. Available on: https://www.nytimes.com/2007/11/11/opinion/11iht-edbrain.1.8281355.html.

"International Statistical Classification of Diseases and Related Health Problems (ICD)." World Health Organization (WHO). Available on: https://www.who.int/standards/classifications/classification-of-diseases.

Jumel, Bernard. *Les Troubles de l'attention chez l'enfant*. Paris: Dunad, 2014.

Kazda, Luise, Katy Bell, Ray Thomas et al. "Overdiagnosis of Attention-Deficit/Hyperactivity Disorder in Children and Adolescents: A Systematic Scoping Review." *JAMA Network Open* 4, no. 4 (2021). Available on: https://jamanetwork.com/journals/jamanetworkopen/fullarticle/2778451.

Kendell, Robert and Assen Jablensky. "Distinguish between the Validity and Utility of Psychiatric Diagnoses." *American Journal of Psychiatry* 160, no. 4 (2003): 4-22.

"Key Findings of the Prevalence of Attention-Deficit/Hyperactivity Disorder: Its Diagnosis and Treatment in a Community Based Epidemologic Study." Center for Disease Control (CDC), 2014. Available on: http://www.cdc.gov/ncbddd/adhd/features/adhd-key-findings-play.html.

Kinderman, Peter. *A Manifesto for Mental Health: Why We Need a Revolution in Mental Health Care*. Switzerland: Springer International Publishing, 2019.

La Bruyère, Jean de. *The Characters, or the Manners of the Age, with the Characters of Theophrastus*. London: Forgotten Books, 2018.

"La Preuve par L'Image." Association canadienne-française pour l'avancement des sciences (ACFAS). Available on: https://www.acfas.ca/prix-concours/preuve-image.

Lacan, Jacques. *Ecrits: The First Complete Edition in English*. Translated by Bruce Fink. New York: W. W. Norton & Company, 2006.

Landman, Patrick. *Tristesse Business, Le scandale du DSM*. Paris: Max Milo, 2013.

Lane, Christopher. *Shyness: How Normal Behavior Became a Sickness*, New Haven: Yale University Press, 2007.

Lebowitz, Mathew S. "Stigmatization of ADHD: A Developmental Review." *Journal of Attention Disorders* 20, no. 3 (2016): 199–205.

"Le CNRS organise le concours *La revue par l'image*." Centre National de la Recherche Scientifique (CNRS). Available on: https://www.concours-preuve-image.fr/a-propos/

Le Heuzey, Marie-France. *L'Adolescent hyperactif*. Paris: Odile Jacob, 2009.

Lignes directrices du Collège des médecins et de l'ordre des psychologies. "Le trouble déficit de l'attention /hyperactivité et l'usage de stimulants du système nerveux central." (September 2001). Available on: https://numerique.banq.qc.ca/patrimoine/details/52327/2484579.

Mahone, E. Mark and Ericka L. Wodka. "The Neurobiological Profile of Girls with ADHD." *Developmental Disabilities Research Reviews* 14 (2008): 276-284.

Mannuzza, Salvatore and Rachel G. Klein. "Long-term Prognosis in Attention-Deficit/Hyperactivity Disorder." *Child and Adolescent Psychiatric Clinics of North America* 9, no. 3 (July 2000): 711-726.

Marzillier, John. "The Myth of Evidence-Based Psychotherapy." *The Psychologist* 47, no. 7 (July 2004): 392-395.

"MedWatch: The FDA Safety Information and Adverse Event Reporting Program." US Food and Drug Administration (FDA). Available on: https://www.fda.gov/safety/medwatch-fda-safety-information-and-adverse-event-reporting-program.

Mellier, Denis. "The Psychic Envelopes in Psychoanalytic Theories of Infancy." *Frontiers in Psychology* 5 (July 15, 2014). Available on: https://www.frontiersin.org/articles/10.3389/fpsyg.2014.

Ménéchal, Jean and Roger Misès. *L'Hyperactivité infantile, Débats et enjeux*. Paris: Dunod, 2004.

Minard, Michel. *Le DSM roi, La Psychiatrie américaine et la fabrique des diagnostics*. Toulouse: Érès, 2013.

Moncrieff, Joanna, Ruth C. Cooper, Tom Stockmann et al. "The Serotonin Theory of Depression: A Systematic Umbrella of the Evidence." *Molecular Psychiatry* (July 2022): 1-14.

Moncrieff, Joanna. *A Straight Talking Introduction to Psychiatric Drugs: The Truth About How They Work and How to Come Off Them.* 2nd edition. United Kingdom: PCCS Books, 2009.

Morrow, Richard L. et al. "Influence of relative age on diagnosis and treatment of attention-deficit/hyperactivity disorder in children." *Canadian Medical Association Journal* 184, no. 7 (April 17, 2012): 755-762. Available on: https://doi.org/10.1503/cmaj.111619.

Moyniham, Ray and Alan Cassels. *Selling Sickness: How the World's Biggest Pharmaceutical Companies Are Turning Us All into Patients.* New York: Nation Books, 2006.

Moynihan, Ray et al. "Too Much Medicine: From Evidence to Action." *BMJ (Clinical research ed.)* (Dec. 2013). Available on: https://doi.org/10.1136/bmj.f7141.

Murray, Henry A. et al. *Thematic Apperception Test (TAT).* New York: Pearson North America, 1973.

Noble, Holcomb B. "Study Backs a Drug for Hyperactive Children." *The New York Times*, Dec. 15, 1999.

Pelham Jr., William and Gregory Fabiano. "Evidence-Based Psychosocial Treatments for Attention-Deficit/Hyperactivity Disorder." *Journal of Clinical Child & Adolescent Psychology* 37, no. 1 (2008):184-214.

Perron, Roger. "How to do research? Reply to Otto Kernberg." *International Journal of Psychoanalysis* 87, pt. 4 (August 2006): 927-37.

"Research Domain Criteria Initiative." National Institute of Mental Health (NIMH). Available on: https://www.nimh.nih.gov/research/research-funded-by-nimh/rdoc.

Rey, Joseph M., Francisco B. Assumpção Jr. et al. "History of Child Psychiatry." *Miscellaneous J.* 10 (2015): 1-72.

Rice, Timothy. "Commentary: How Child's Play Impacts Executive Function-Related Behaviors." *Frontiers in Psychology* 7 (2016). Available on: https://www.frontiersin.org/articles/10.3389/fpsyg.2016.00968.

Roudinesco, Elisabeth. *Philosophes dans la tourmente*. Paris: Fayard, 2005.

Saul, Richard. *ADHD Does Not Exist: The Truth About Attention Deficit and Hyperactivity Disorder*. New York: HarperWave, 2014.

Schowalter, John E., MD. "A History of Child and Adolescent Psychiatry in the United States." *Psychiatric Times* 20, no. 9 (September 1, 2003). Available on: https://www.psychiatrictimes.com/view/history-child-and-adolescent-psychiatry-united-states.

Schwarz, Alan. *ADHD Nation: Children, Doctors, Big Pharma, and the Making of an American Epidemic*. New York: Scribner, 2017.

Shannon, Scott M. *Mental Health for the Whole Child: Moving Young Clients from Disease*. New York: W.W. Norton and Co., 2013.

Shorter, Edward. *A History of Psychiatry: From the Era of the Asylum to the Age of Prozac*. New York: John Wiley and Sons, 1998.

Smith, Matthew. *Hyperactive: The Controversial History of ADHD*. London: Reaktion Books, 2013.

St-Onge, Jean-Claude. *Tous fous? L'influence de l'industrie pharmaceutique sur la psychiatrie*. Montreal: Ecosociété, 2013.

Strauss, Sharon E. and W. Scott Richardson. *Evidence-Based Medicine*. 4th edition. New York: Elsevier, 2007.

Supporting Emotional Needs of the Gifted (SENG). Available on: https://www.sengifted.org/

Swain, Gladys and Marcel Gauchet. *Le Sujet de la folie*. Paris: Calmann-Lévy, 1997.

Szasz, Thomas. *The Myth of Mental Illness: Foundations of a Theory of Personal Conduct*. New York: Harper & Row, 1974.

Szwec, Gérard. "Les procédés autocalmants pour la recherche répétitive de l'excitation (les galériens volontaires)." *Revue française de psychosomatique* 4, no. 1 (1993): 27-51.

Tallis, Raymond. *Aping Mankind: Neuromania, Darwinitis and the Misrepresentation of Humanity*. United Kingdom: Taylor & Francis, 2016.

"More U.S. Children Being Diagnosed with Youthful Tendency Disorder." *The Onion*, September 27, 2000. Available on: https://www.theonion.com/more-u-s-children-being-diagnosed-with-youthful-tenden-1819565754.

Timimi, Sami and Eric Taylor. "ADHD is Best Understood as a Cultural Construct." *The British Journal of Psychiatry* 84, no. 1 (2003): 8-9.

"Trouble déficit de l'attention avec ou sans hyperactivité (TDAH): repérer la souffrance, accompagner l'enfant et la famille." Haute Autorité de Santé (HAS). February 15, 2015. Available on: https://www.has-sante.fr/jcms/c_2012647/fr/trouble-deficit-de-l-attention-avec-ou-sans-hyperactivite-tdah-reperer-la-souffrance-accompagner-l-enfant-et-la-famille.

Scheffler, Richard M., Timothy Brown et al. "Positive Association Between Attention-Deficit/Hyperactivity Disorder Medication Use and Academic Achievement During Elementary School." *Pediatrics* 123, no. 5 (2009): 1273–79.

Toannidis, John P. "Why Most Published Research Findings Are False." *PLoSMedicine* 2, no. 8 (August 2005): 696-701.

Vidya L. Nathan. "Alcobra ADHD Drug Meets Goals, after Excluding Some Data." *Reuters Health News*. Oct 7, 2014. Available on: http://www.psychcongress.com/article/alcobras-adhd-drug-meets-goals-after-excluding-some-data-19233.

Virapen, John. *Side Effects: Death. Confessions of a Pharma-Insider.* Texas: Virtualbookworm.com Publishing, 2010.

Wechsler, David. *Weschler Intelligence Scale for Children*. 3rd edition. San Antonio, TX: The Psychological Corporation, 1991.

Whitaker, Robert. *Anatomy of an Epidemic: Magic Bullets, Psychiatric Drugs, and the Astonishing Rise of Mental Illness in America*. New York: Crown, 2010.

Willoughby, Michael T. and Patrick J. Curran. "Implications of Latent Trajectory Models for the Study of Developmental Psychopathology." *Development and Psychopathology* 15, (2003): 581-612.

Wingfield, Nick, and Conor Dougherty. "Drug Testing Is Coming to E-Sports." *The New York Times*, July 23, 2015. Available on: https://www.nytimes.com/2015/07/24/technology/drug-testing-is-coming-to-e-gaming.html.

Winnicott, Donald W. *Through Paediatrics to Psychoanalysis: Collected Papers.* London: Karnac, 1984 [1956].

Yoder Keith J., and Jean Decety. "The Neuroscience of Morality and Social Decision-Making." *Psychology, Crime, and Law* 24, no. 3 (2018): 279-295.

Zeki, Semir. *Inner Vision: An Exploration of Art and the Brain.* Oxford and New York: Oxford University Press, 1999.

Titles Published by The Sea Horse Imprint:

Betty Bernardo Fuks — *Freud and the Invention of Jewishness* (2008)

Gérard Haddad — *Eating the Book: Dietary Rites and Paternal Function* (2013)

Erik Porge — *Truth and Knowledge in the Clinic: Working with Freud and Lacan* (2016)

Paola Mieli — *Figures of Space: Subject, Body, Place* (2017)

Alain Didier-Weill — *The Three Times of the Law* (2017)

Marie-Magdeleine Lessana — *Marilyn: Portrait of a Shooting Star* (2019)

Jean-Pierre Cléro — *Lacan and the English Language* (2020)

Patrick Landman — *Are We All Hyperactive? The Astonishing Epidemic of Attention Disorders* (2024)

www.ingramcontent.com/pod-product-compliance
Lightning Source LLC
Chambersburg PA
CBHW022058020426
42335CB00012B/743